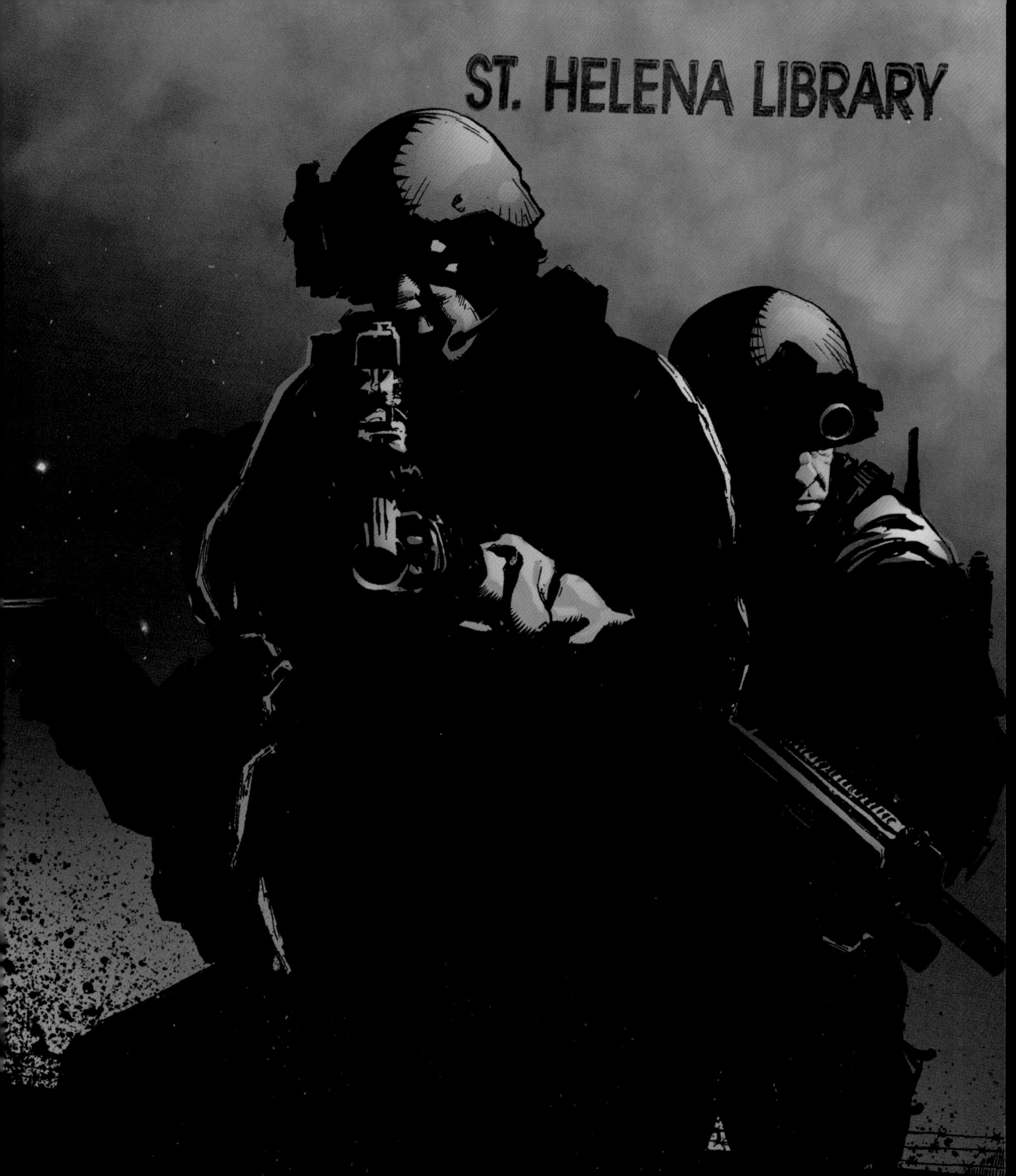

CODE WORD: GERONIMO

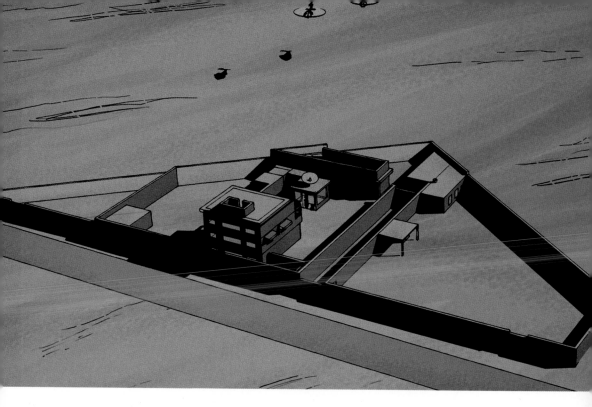

WRITTEN BY CAPTAIN DALE DYE (USMC, RET)
AND JULIA DYE PH.D.

ART BY GERRY KISSELL • AMIN AMAT

AFTERWORD BY JOHN M. DEL VECCHIO

Inks by Amin Amat and David Enebral • Colors by: Ruben Cubiles and Gerry Kissell
Additional Colors by: Marc Rueda, Alex Towers, Miquel Diaz, Lucrecia Fraile, Ego, and Nieves Fernández
Editor: Tom Waltz • Lettering: Robbie Robbins

I dedicate my work on this book to every person in uniform who served in this war, and especially to Seal Team Six... thank you. I also want to thank my children, Ben, Zoe and Sean, for all their love, support and faith in me. Another special thank you goes to Tyler Button, for planting the seed in my head that became this book.

– Gerry Kissell

Special thanks from IDW Publishing and Charlie Foxtrot Entertainment to Peter Zaragoza and Eduardo Alpuente for their invaluable assistance in the creation of this graphic novel.

ISBN: 978-1-61377-097-9

14 13 12 11 1 2 3 4

IDW®

Ted Adams, CEO & Publisher
Greg Goldstein, Chief Operating Officer
Robbie Robbins, EVP/Sr. Graphic Artist
Chris Ryall, Chief Creative Officer/Editor-in-Chief
Matthew Ruzicka, CPA, Chief Financial Officer
Alan Payne, VP of Sales

Become our fan on Facebook **facebook.com/idwpublishing**
Follow us on Twitter **@idwpublishing**
Check us out on YouTube **youtube.com/idwpublishing**
www.IDWPUBLISHING.com

CODE WORD: GERONIMO. SEPTEMBER 2011. FIRST PRINTING.

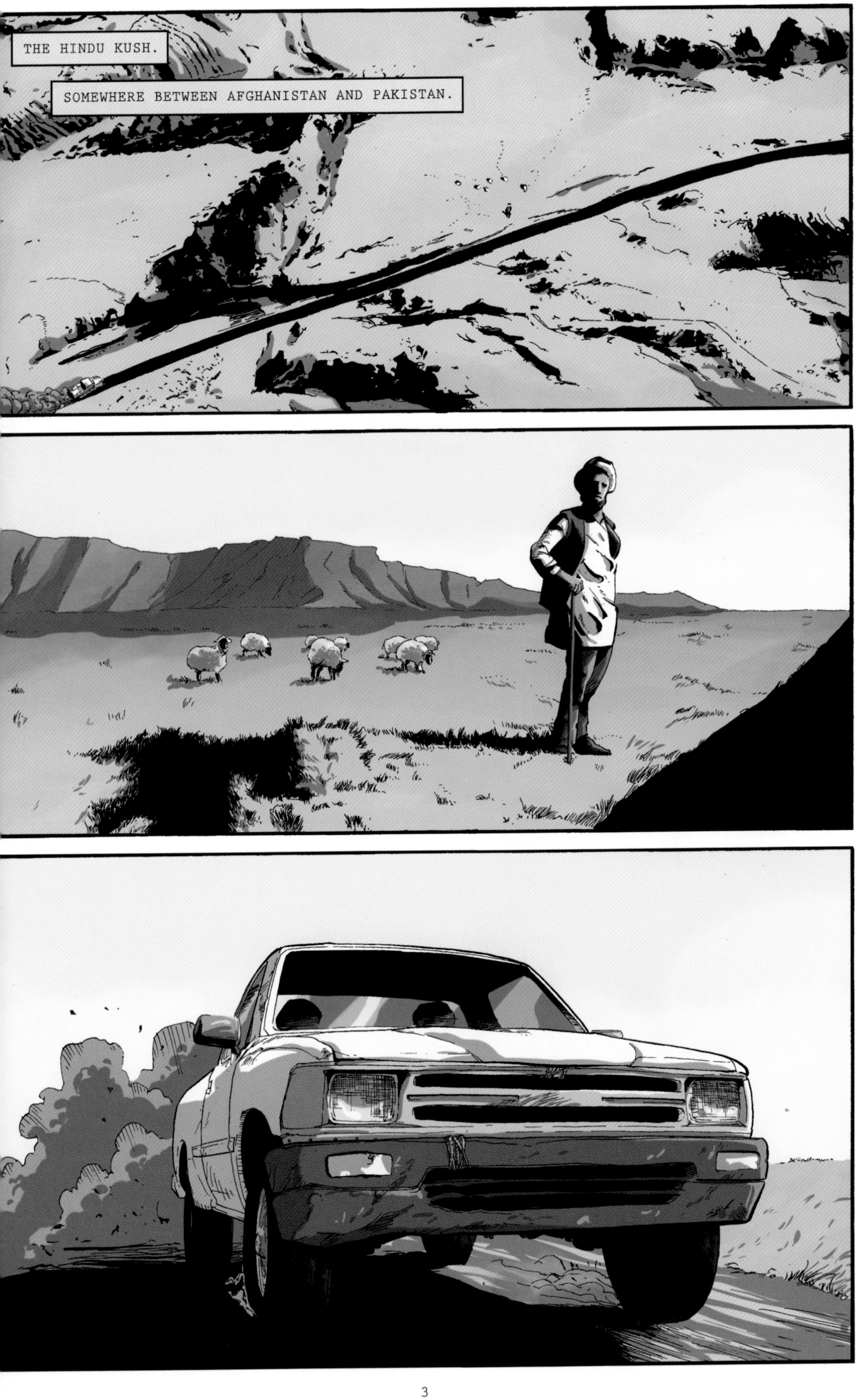
THE HINDU KUSH.
SOMEWHERE BETWEEN AFGHANISTAN AND PAKISTAN.

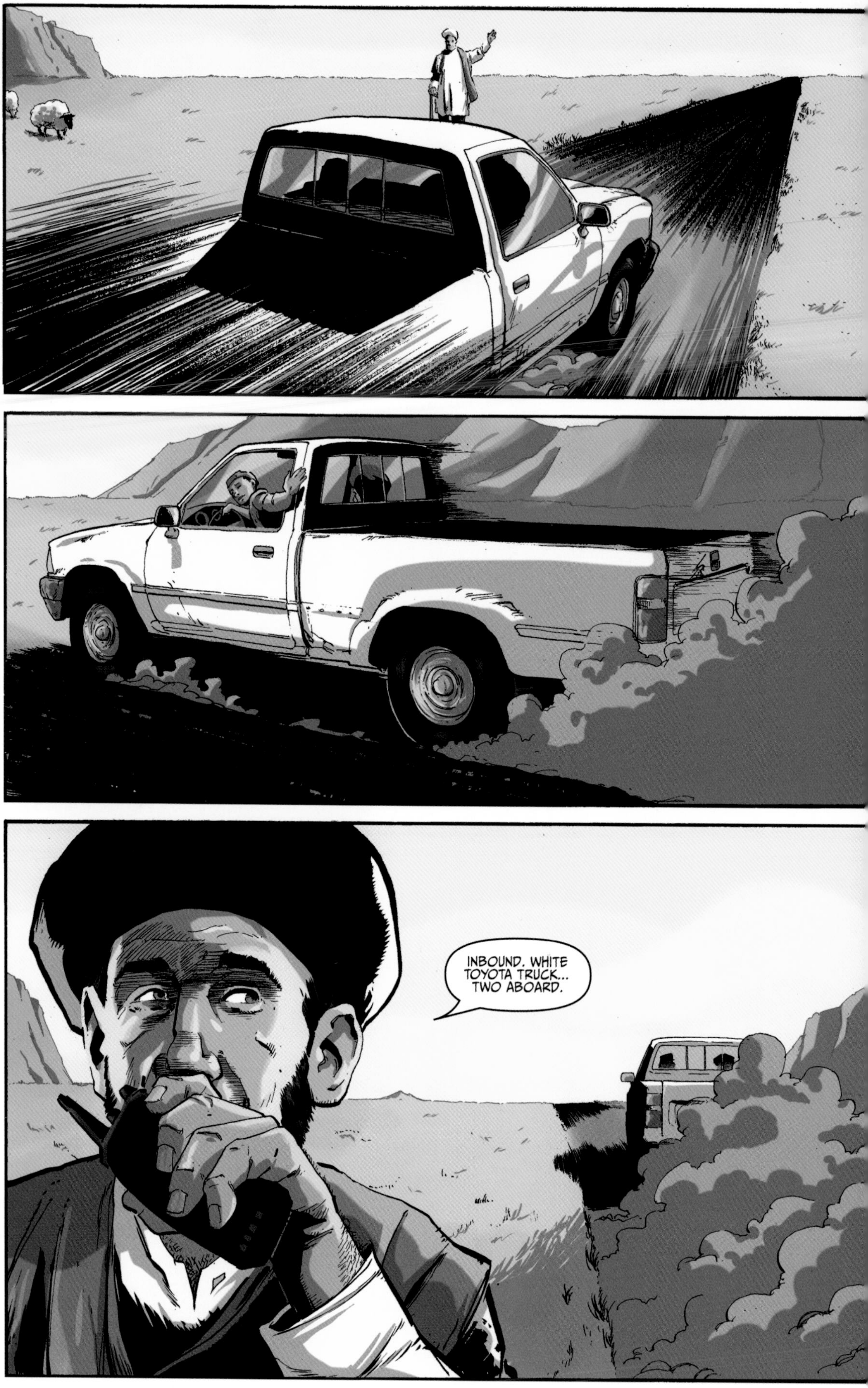
INBOUND. WHITE TOYOTA TRUCK... TWO ABOARD.

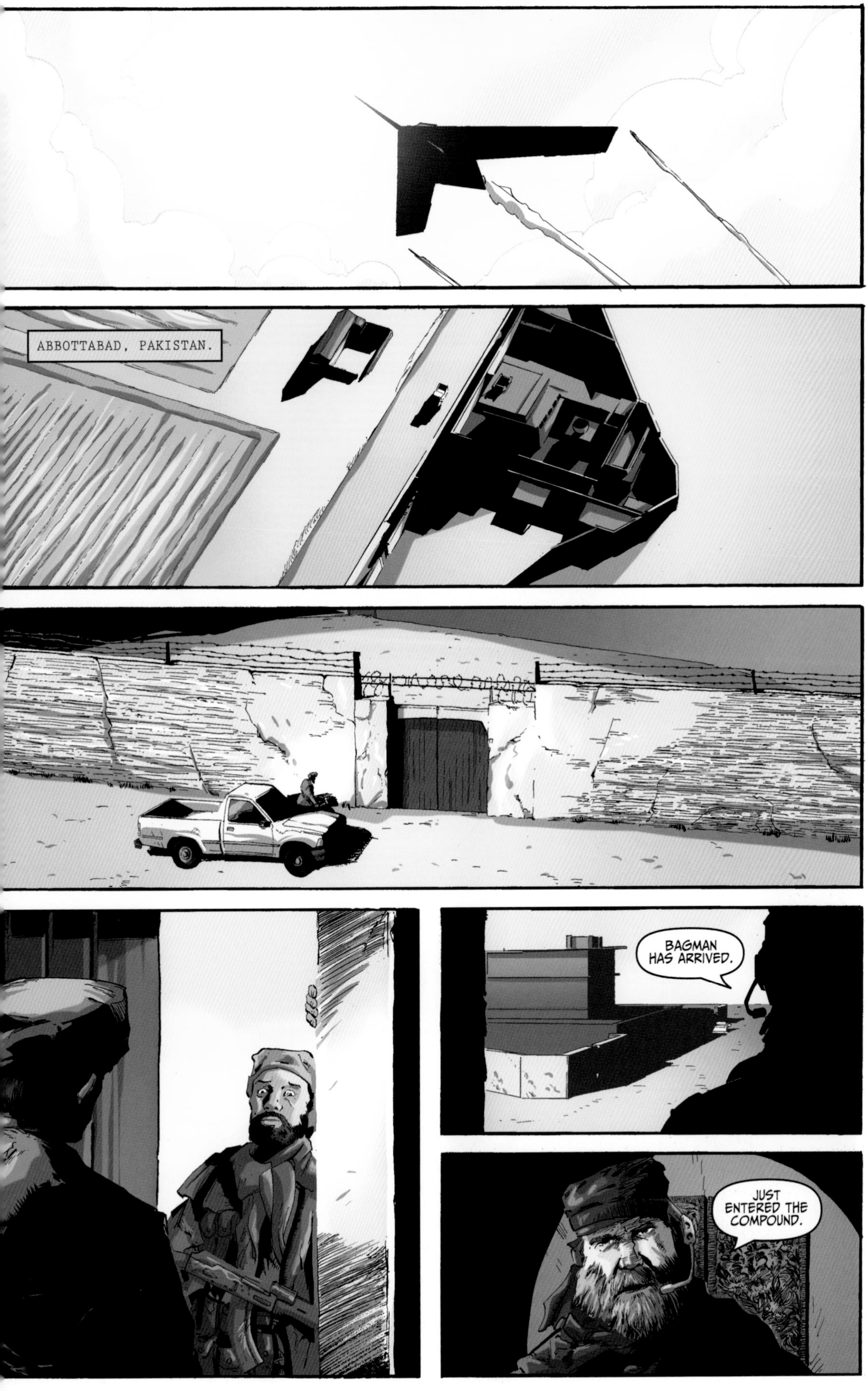
ABBOTTABAD, PAKISTAN.
BAGMAN HAS ARRIVED.
JUST ENTERED THE COMPOUND.

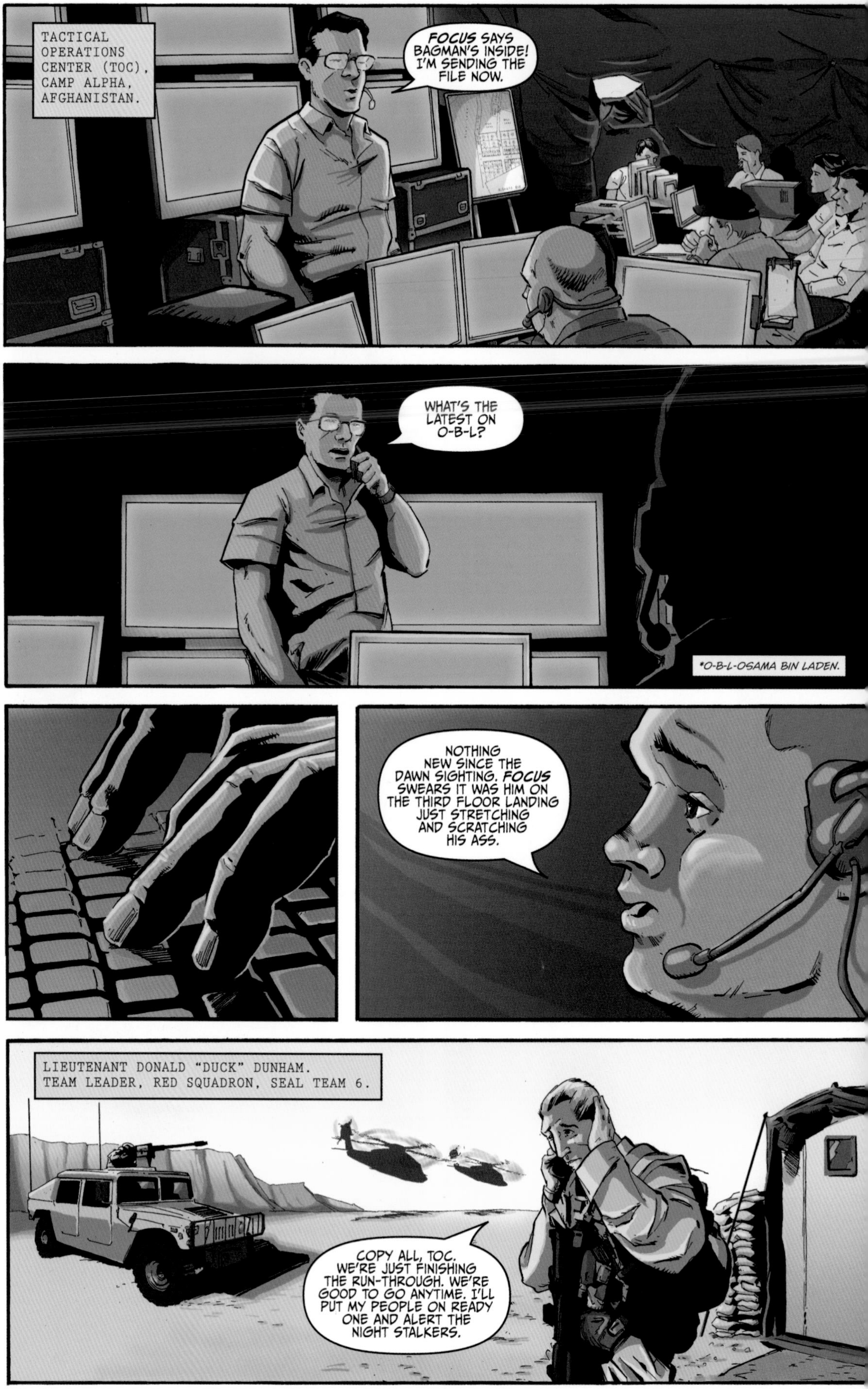
TACTICAL OPERATIONS CENTER (TOC), CAMP ALPHA, AFGHANISTAN.
FOCUS SAYS BAGMAN'S INSIDE! I'M SENDING THE FILE NOW.
WHAT'S THE LATEST ON O-B-L?
*O-B-L-OSAMA BIN LADEN.
NOTHING NEW SINCE THE DAWN SIGHTING. FOCUS SWEARS IT WAS HIM ON THE THIRD FLOOR LANDING JUST STRETCHING AND SCRATCHING HIS ASS.
LIEUTENANT DONALD "DUCK" DUNHAM. TEAM LEADER, RED SQUADRON, SEAL TEAM 6.
COPY ALL, TOC. WE'RE JUST FINISHING THE RUN-THROUGH. WE'RE GOOD TO GO ANYTIME. I'LL PUT MY PEOPLE ON READY ONE AND ALERT THE NIGHT STALKERS.

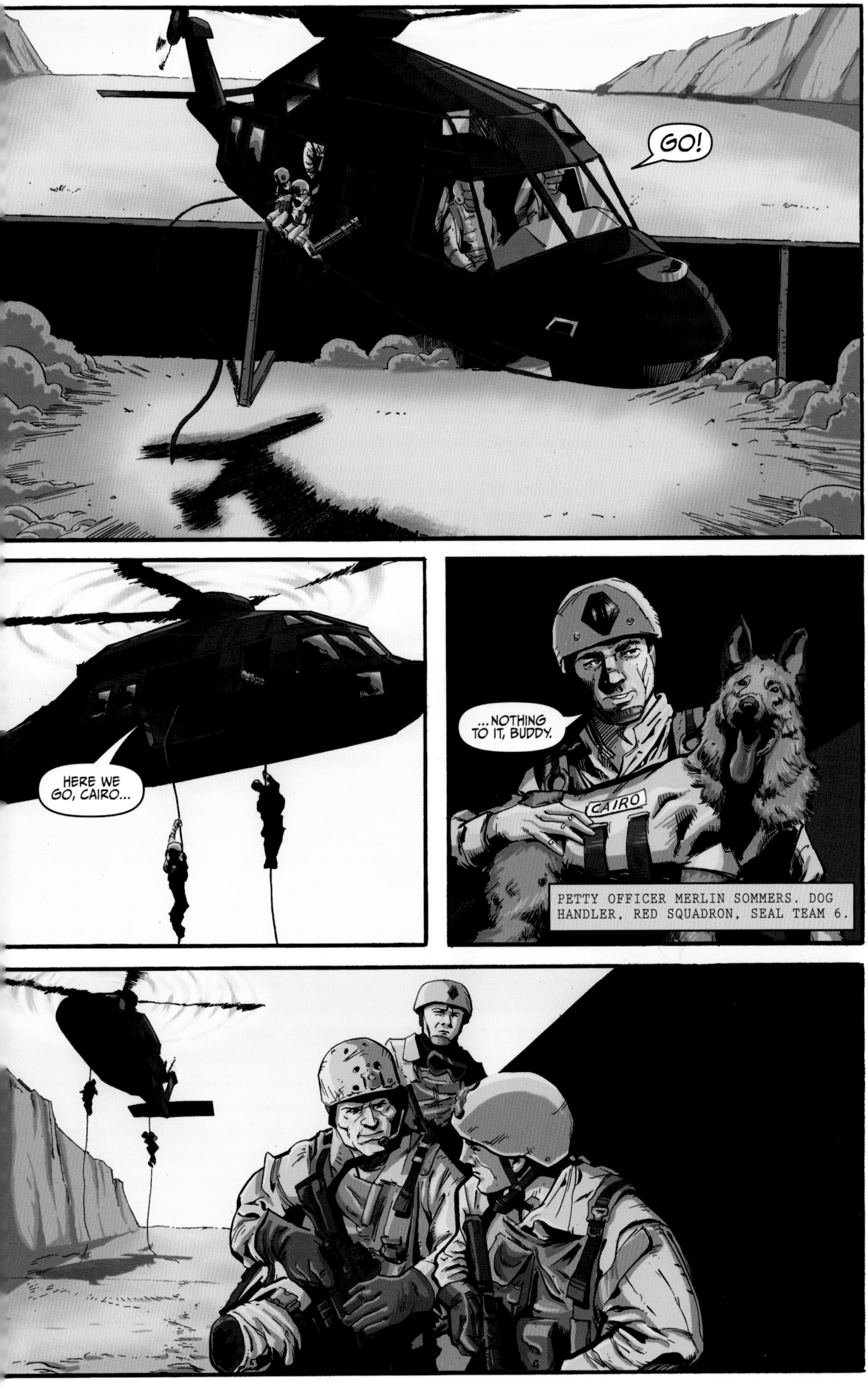
GO!
HERE WE GO, CAIRO...
...NOTHING TO IT, BUDDY.
CAIRO
PETTY OFFICER MERLIN SOMMERS. DOG HANDLER, RED SQUADRON, SEAL TEAM 6.

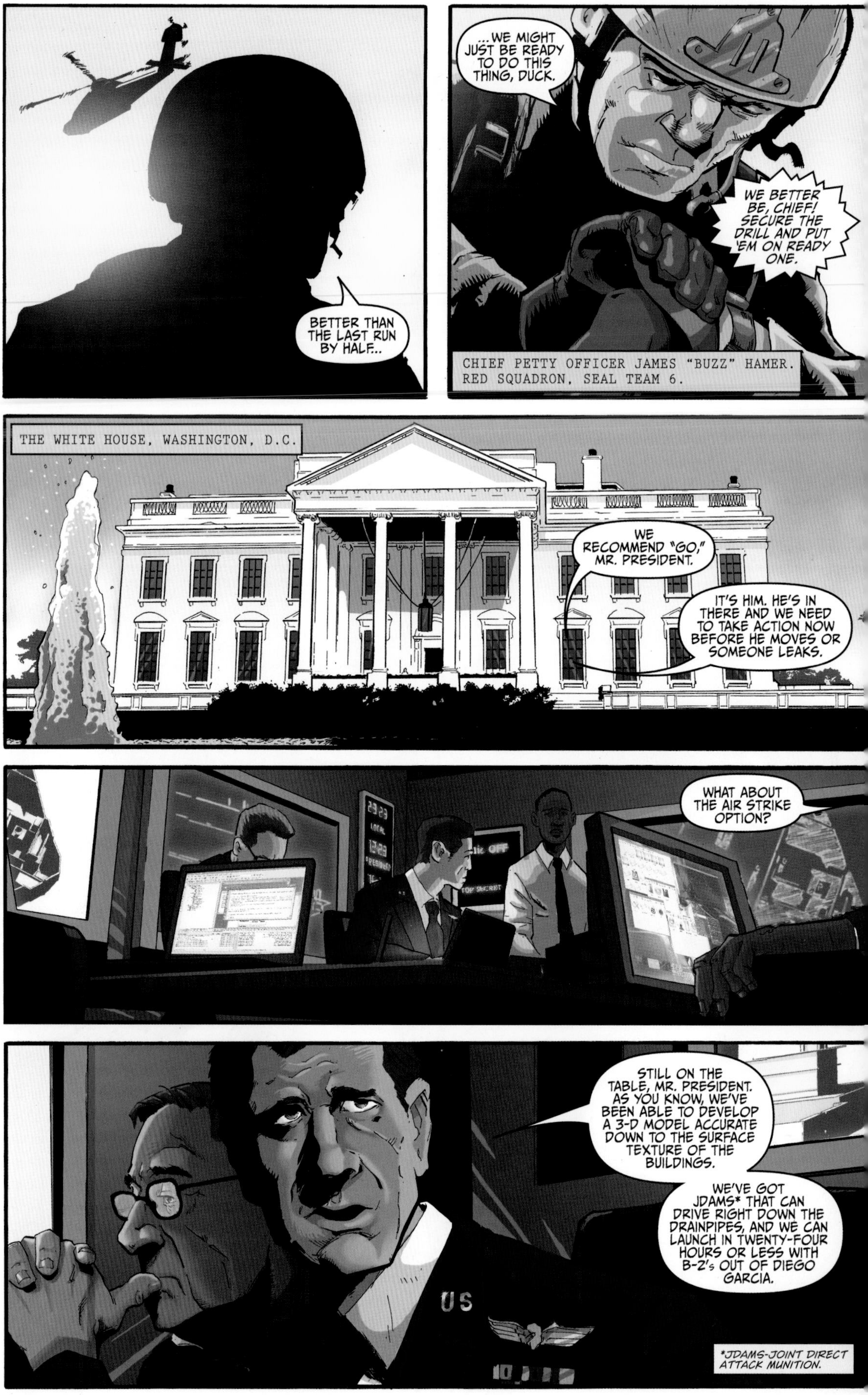
BETTER THAN THE LAST RUN BY HALF...
...WE MIGHT JUST BE READY TO DO THIS THING, DUCK.
WE BETTER BE, CHIEF! SECURE THE DRILL AND PUT 'EM ON READY ONE.
CHIEF PETTY OFFICER JAMES "BUZZ" HAMER. RED SQUADRON, SEAL TEAM 6.
THE WHITE HOUSE, WASHINGTON, D.C.
WE RECOMMEND "GO," MR. PRESIDENT.
IT'S HIM. HE'S IN THERE AND WE NEED TO TAKE ACTION NOW BEFORE HE MOVES OR SOMEONE LEAKS.
WHAT ABOUT THE AIR STRIKE OPTION?
STILL ON THE TABLE, MR. PRESIDENT. AS YOU KNOW, WE'VE BEEN ABLE TO DEVELOP A 3-D MODEL ACCURATE DOWN TO THE SURFACE TEXTURE OF THE BUILDINGS.
WE'VE GOT JDAMS* THAT CAN DRIVE RIGHT DOWN THE DRAINPIPES, AND WE CAN LAUNCH IN TWENTY-FOUR HOURS OR LESS WITH B-2's OUT OF DIEGO GARCIA.
*JDAMS-JOINT DIRECT ATTACK MUNITION.

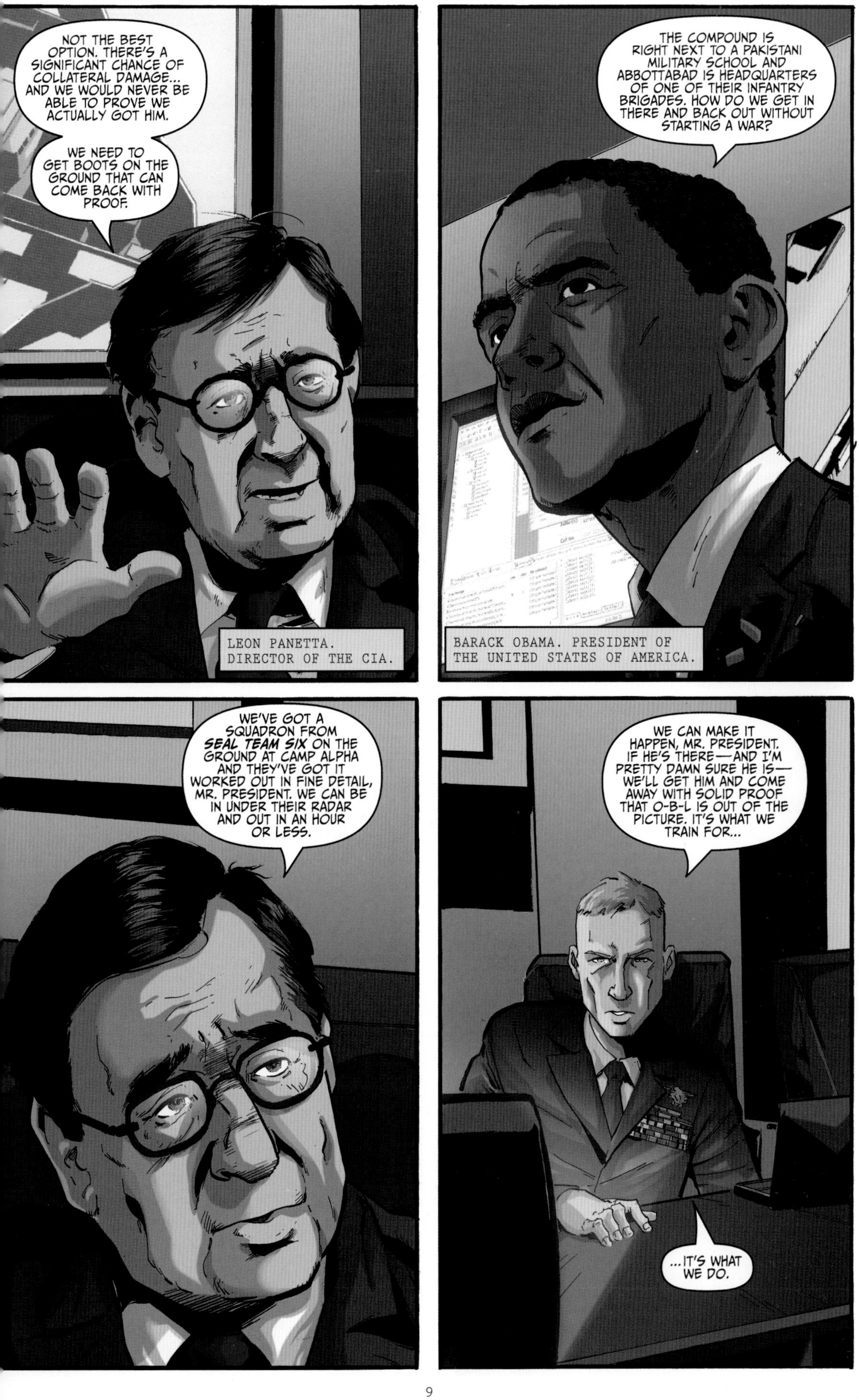
NOT THE BEST OPTION. THERE'S A SIGNIFICANT CHANCE OF COLLATERAL DAMAGE... AND WE WOULD NEVER BE ABLE TO PROVE WE ACTUALLY GOT HIM.
WE NEED TO GET BOOTS ON THE GROUND THAT CAN COME BACK WITH PROOF.
LEON PANETTA. DIRECTOR OF THE CIA.
THE COMPOUND IS RIGHT NEXT TO A PAKISTANI MILITARY SCHOOL AND ABBOTTABAD IS HEADQUARTERS OF ONE OF THEIR INFANTRY BRIGADES. HOW DO WE GET IN THERE AND BACK OUT WITHOUT STARTING A WAR?
BARACK OBAMA. PRESIDENT OF THE UNITED STATES OF AMERICA.
WE'VE GOT A SQUADRON FROM SEAL TEAM SIX ON THE GROUND AT CAMP ALPHA AND THEY'VE GOT IT WORKED OUT IN FINE DETAIL, MR. PRESIDENT. WE CAN BE IN UNDER THEIR RADAR AND OUT IN AN HOUR OR LESS.
WE CAN MAKE IT HAPPEN, MR. PRESIDENT. IF HE'S THERE—AND I'M PRETTY DAMN SURE HE IS—WE'LL GET HIM AND COME AWAY WITH SOLID PROOF THAT O-B-L IS OUT OF THE PICTURE. IT'S WHAT WE TRAIN FOR...
...IT'S WHAT WE DO.

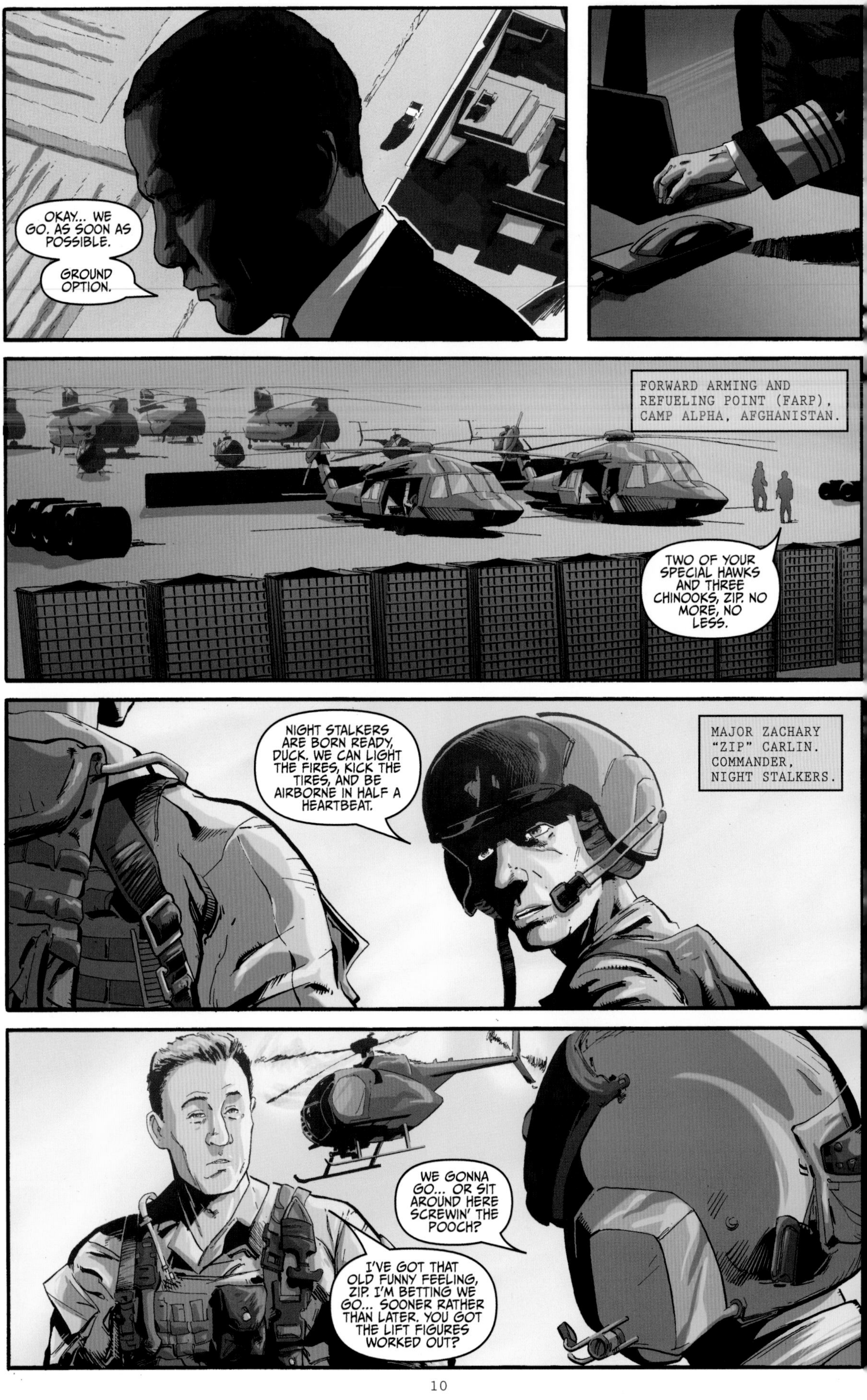
OKAY... WE GO. AS SOON AS POSSIBLE.
GROUND OPTION.
FORWARD ARMING AND REFUELING POINT (FARP), CAMP ALPHA, AFGHANISTAN.
TWO OF YOUR SPECIAL HAWKS AND THREE CHINOOKS, ZIP. NO MORE, NO LESS.
NIGHT STALKERS ARE BORN READY, DUCK. WE CAN LIGHT THE FIRES, KICK THE TIRES, AND BE AIRBORNE IN HALF A HEARTBEAT.
MAJOR ZACHARY "ZIP" CARLIN. COMMANDER, NIGHT STALKERS.
WE GONNA GO... OR SIT AROUND HERE SCREWIN' THE POOCH?
I'VE GOT THAT OLD FUNNY FEELING, ZIP. I'M BETTING WE GO... SOONER RATHER THAN LATER. YOU GOT THE LIFT FIGURES WORKED OUT?

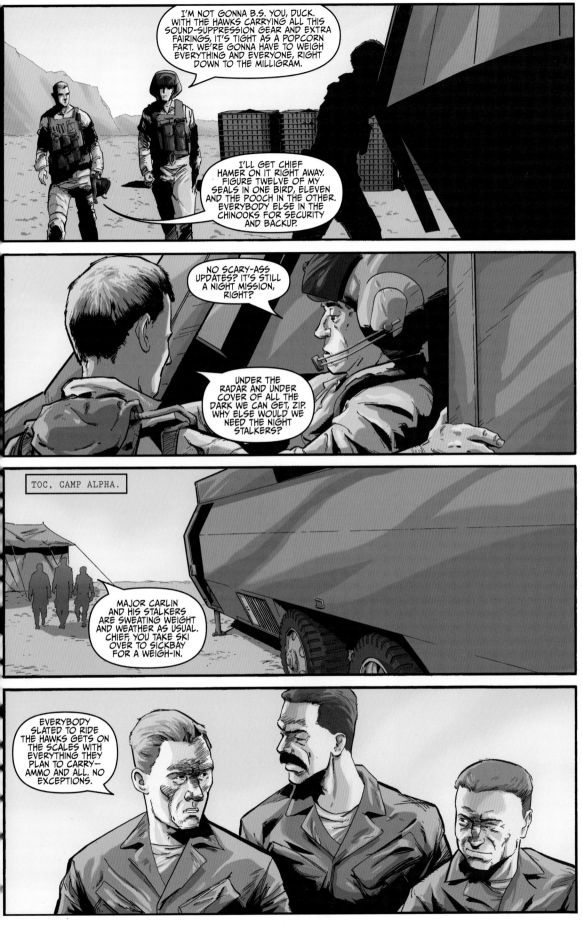

I'M NOT GONNA B.S. YOU, DUCK. WITH THE HAWKS CARRYING ALL THIS SOUND-SUPPRESSION GEAR AND EXTRA FAIRINGS, IT'S TIGHT AS A POPCORN FART. WE'RE GONNA HAVE TO WEIGH EVERYTHING AND EVERYONE, RIGHT DOWN TO THE MILLIGRAM.

I'LL GET CHIEF HAMER ON IT RIGHT AWAY. FIGURE TWELVE OF MY SEALS IN ONE BIRD, ELEVEN AND THE POOCH IN THE OTHER. EVERYBODY ELSE IN THE CHINOOKS FOR SECURITY AND BACKUP.

NO SCARY-ASS UPDATES? IT'S STILL A NIGHT MISSION, RIGHT?

UNDER THE RADAR AND UNDER COVER OF ALL THE DARK WE CAN GET, ZIP. WHY ELSE WOULD WE NEED THE NIGHT STALKERS?

TOC, CAMP ALPHA.

MAJOR CARLIN AND HIS STALKERS ARE SWEATING WEIGHT AND WEATHER AS USUAL. CHIEF, YOU TAKE SKI OVER TO SICKBAY FOR A WEIGH-IN.

EVERYBODY SLATED TO RIDE THE HAWKS GETS ON THE SCALES WITH EVERYTHING THEY PLAN TO CARRY—AMMO AND ALL. NO EXCEPTIONS.

11

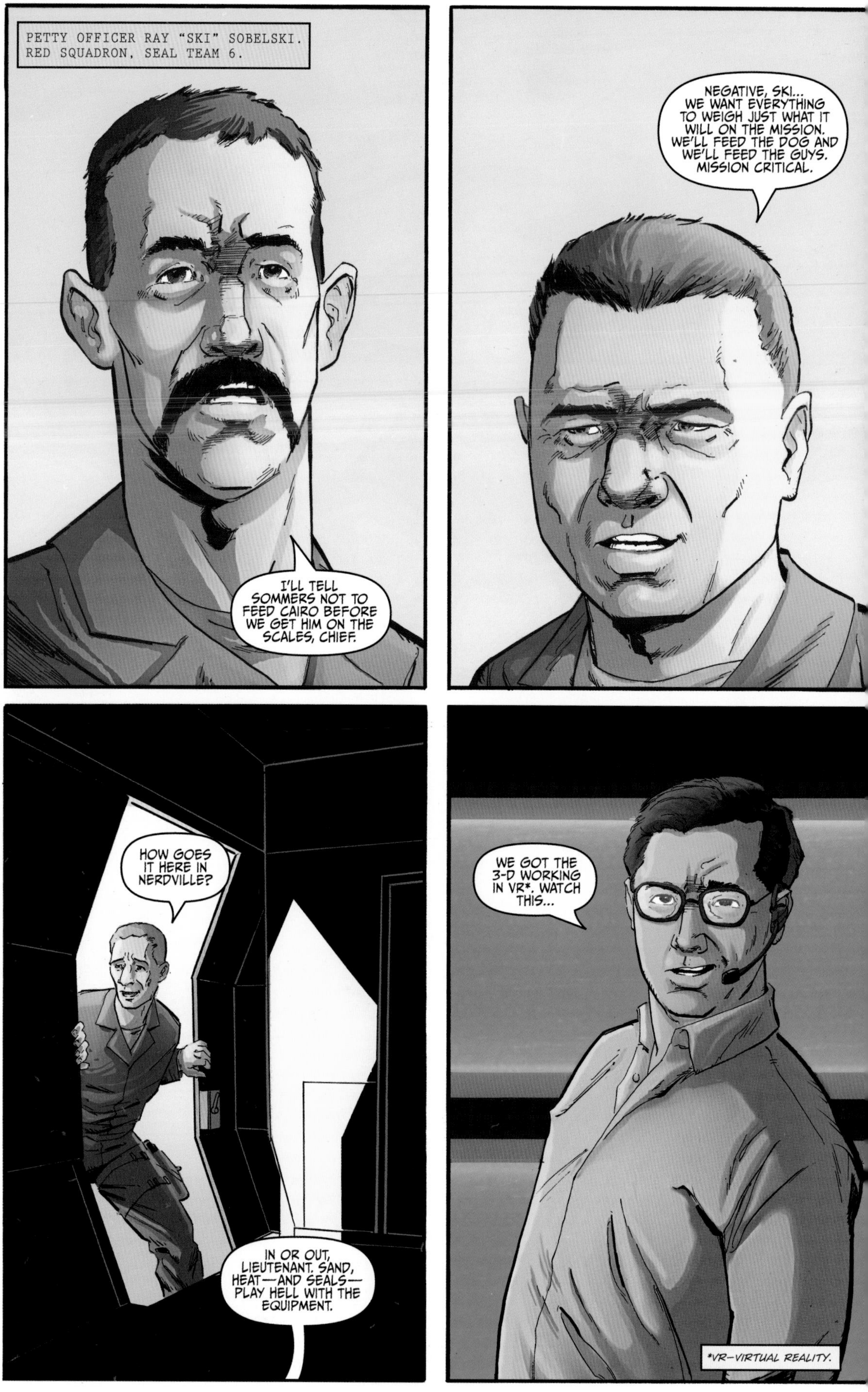
PETTY OFFICER RAY "SKI" SOBELSKI. RED SQUADRON, SEAL TEAM 6.
I'LL TELL SOMMERS NOT TO FEED CAIRO BEFORE WE GET HIM ON THE SCALES, CHIEF.
NEGATIVE, SKI... WE WANT EVERYTHING TO WEIGH JUST WHAT IT WILL ON THE MISSION. WE'LL FEED THE DOG AND WE'LL FEED THE GUYS. MISSION CRITICAL.
HOW GOES IT HERE IN NERDVILLE?
IN OR OUT, LIEUTENANT. SAND, HEAT—AND SEALS—PLAY HELL WITH THE EQUIPMENT.
WE GOT THE 3-D WORKING IN VR*. WATCH THIS...
*VR—VIRTUAL REALITY.

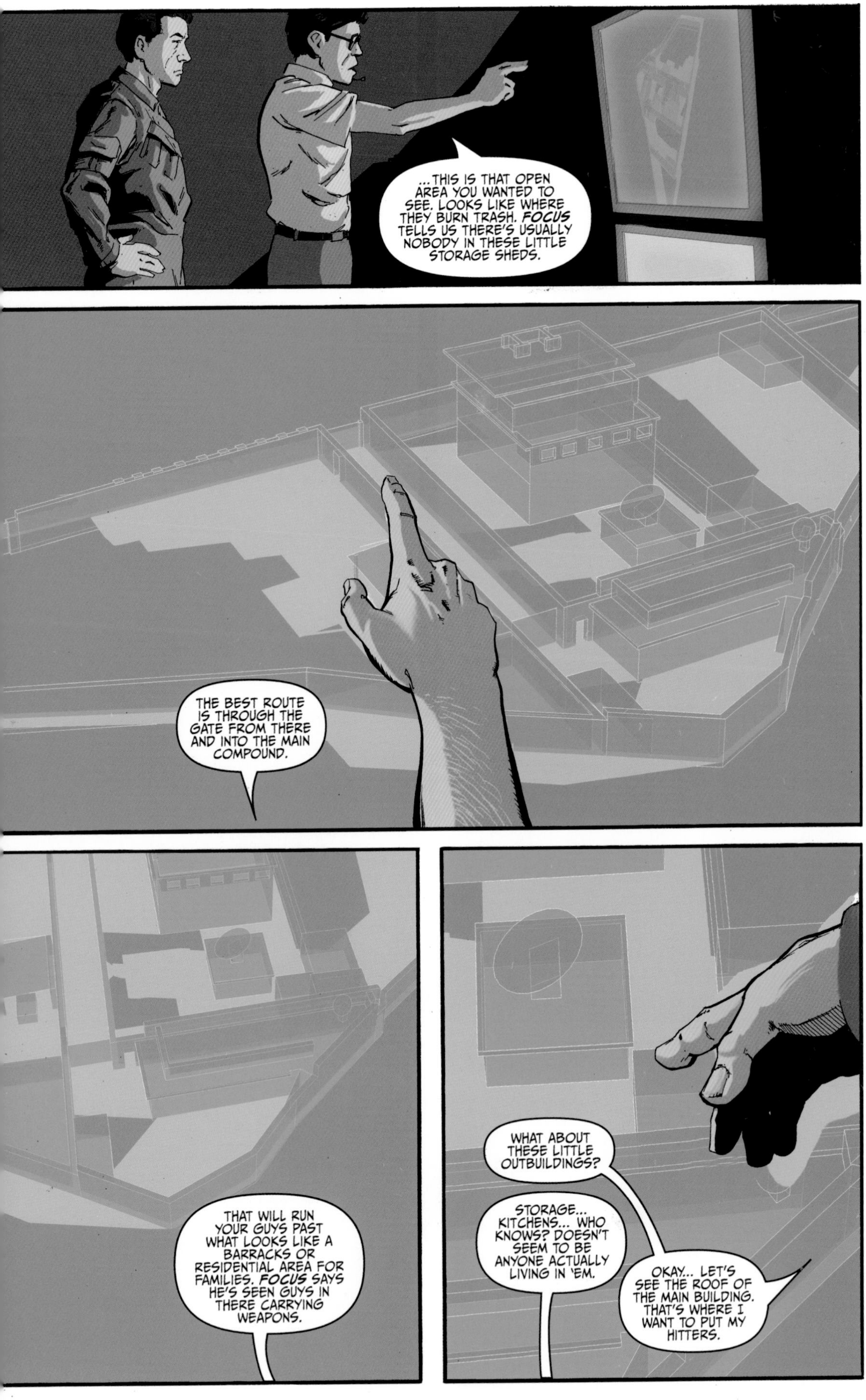
...THIS IS THAT OPEN AREA YOU WANTED TO SEE. LOOKS LIKE WHERE THEY BURN TRASH. *FOCUS* TELLS US THERE'S USUALLY NOBODY IN THESE LITTLE STORAGE SHEDS.
THE BEST ROUTE IS THROUGH THE GATE FROM THERE AND INTO THE MAIN COMPOUND.
THAT WILL RUN YOUR GUYS PAST WHAT LOOKS LIKE A BARRACKS OR RESIDENTIAL AREA FOR FAMILIES. *FOCUS* SAYS HE'S SEEN GUYS IN THERE CARRYING WEAPONS.
WHAT ABOUT THESE LITTLE OUTBUILDINGS?
STORAGE... KITCHENS... WHO KNOWS? DOESN'T SEEM TO BE ANYONE ACTUALLY LIVING IN 'EM.
OKAY... LET'S SEE THE ROOF OF THE MAIN BUILDING. THAT'S WHERE I WANT TO PUT MY HITTERS.

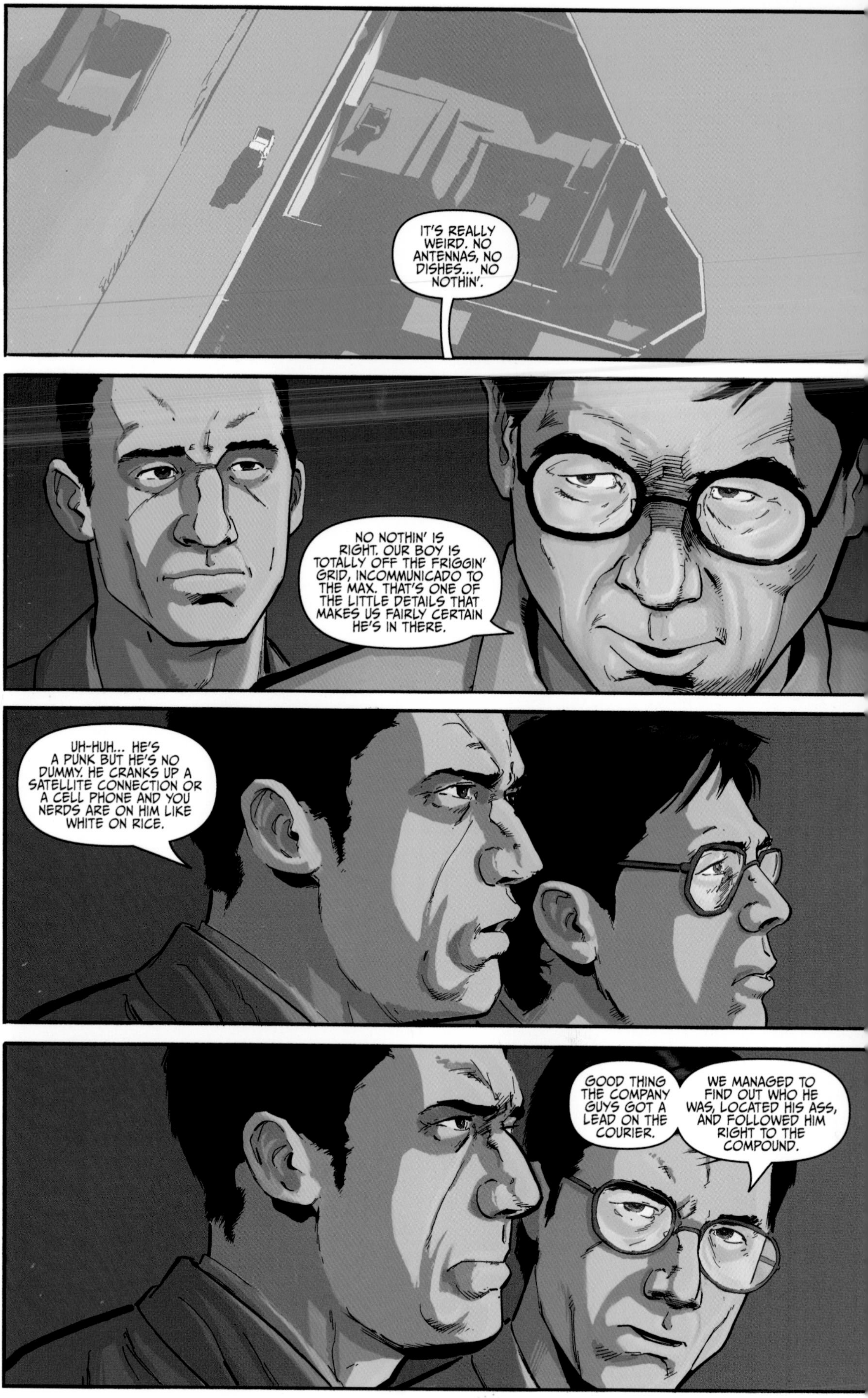
IT'S REALLY WEIRD. NO ANTENNAS, NO DISHES... NO NOTHIN'.
NO NOTHIN' IS RIGHT. OUR BOY IS TOTALLY OFF THE FRIGGIN' GRID, INCOMMUNICADO TO THE MAX. THAT'S ONE OF THE LITTLE DETAILS THAT MAKES US FAIRLY CERTAIN HE'S IN THERE.
UH-HUH... HE'S A PUNK BUT HE'S NO DUMMY. HE CRANKS UP A SATELLITE CONNECTION OR A CELL PHONE AND YOU NERDS ARE ON HIM LIKE WHITE ON RICE.
GOOD THING THE COMPANY GUYS GOT A LEAD ON THE COURIER.
WE MANAGED TO FIND OUT WHO HE WAS, LOCATED HIS ASS, AND FOLLOWED HIM RIGHT TO THE COMPOUND.

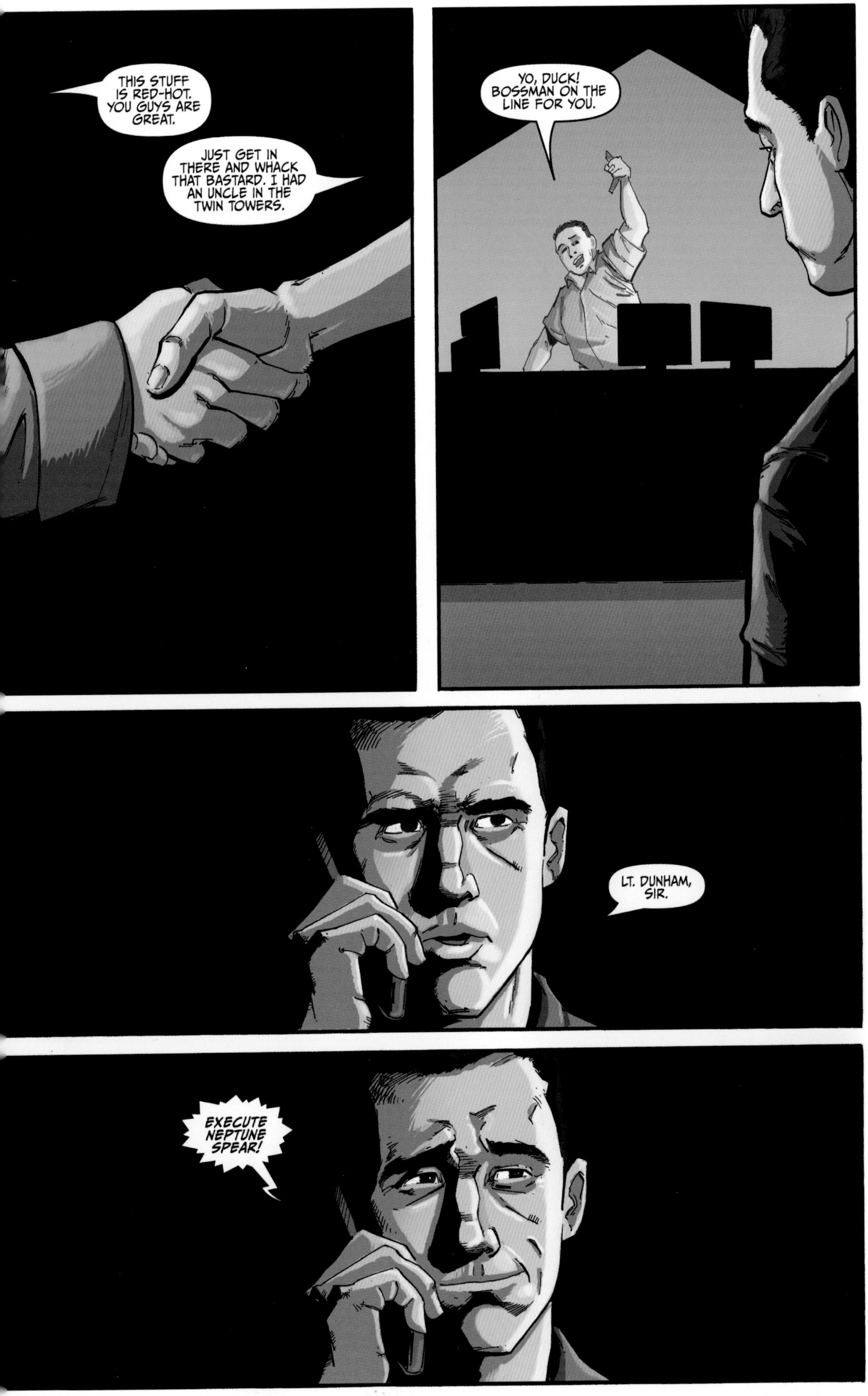
THIS STUFF IS RED-HOT. YOU GUYS ARE GREAT.
JUST GET IN THERE AND WHACK THAT BASTARD. I HAD AN UNCLE IN THE TWIN TOWERS.
YO, DUCK! BOSSMAN ON THE LINE FOR YOU.
LT. DUNHAM, SIR.
EXECUTE NEPTUNE SPEAR!

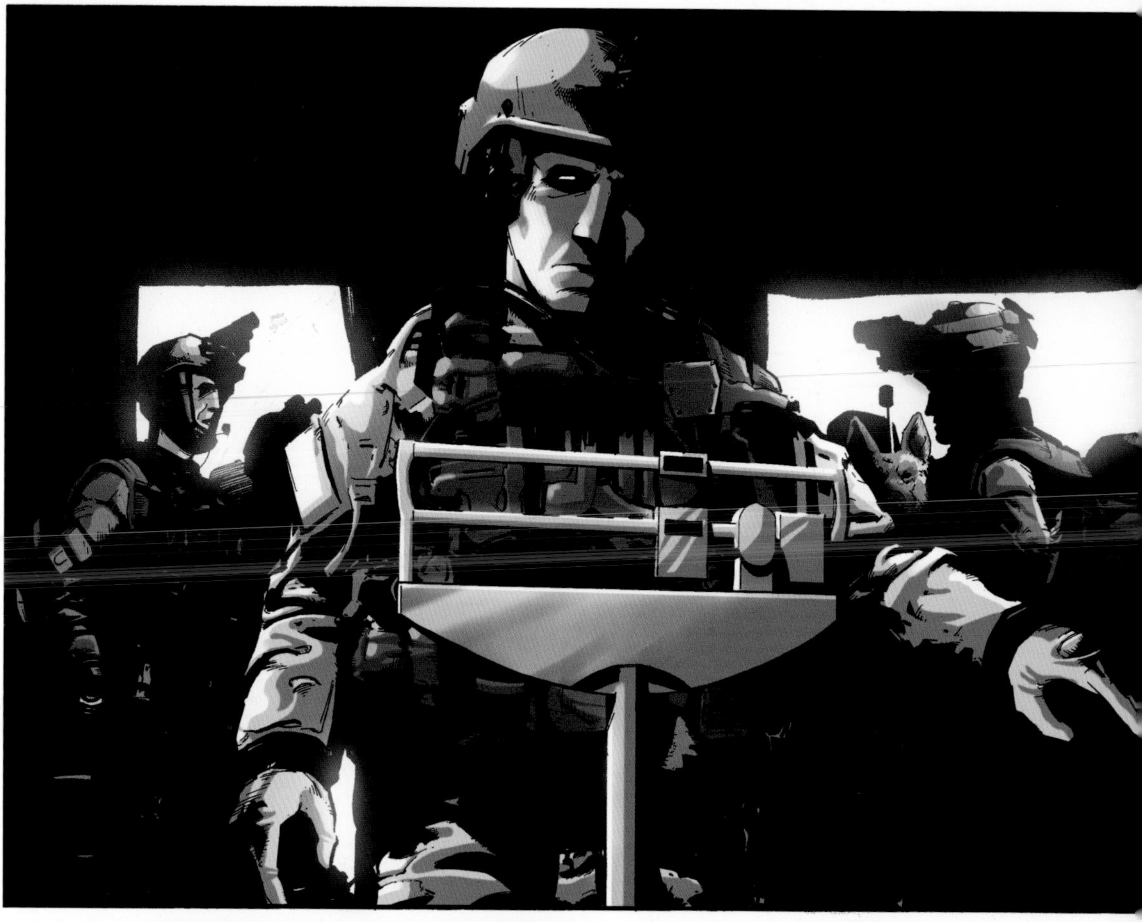

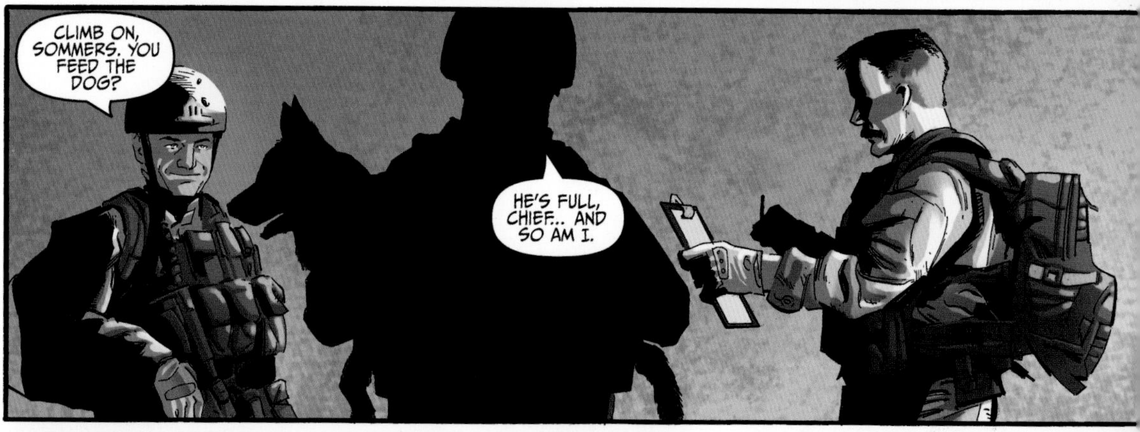
CLIMB ON, SOMMERS. YOU FEED THE DOG?
HE'S FULL, CHIEF... AND SO AM I.

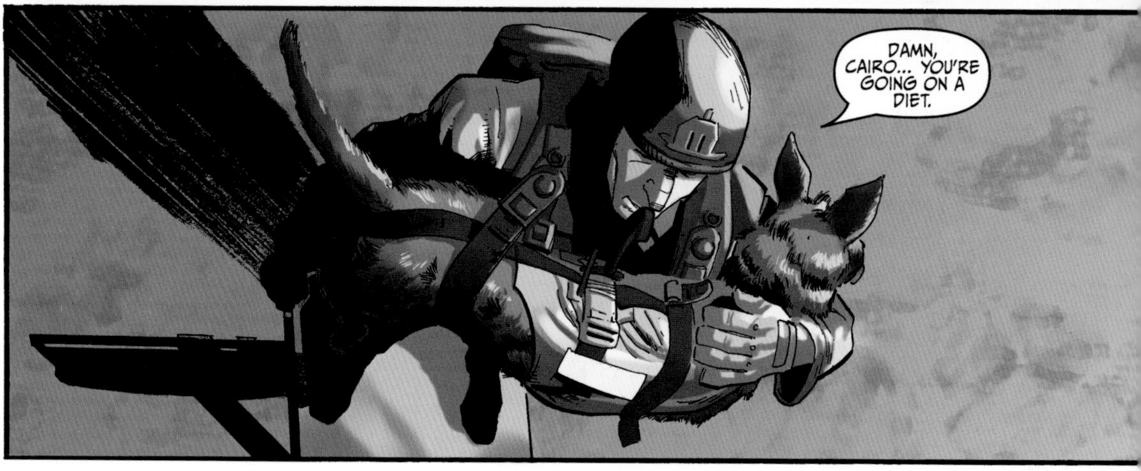
DAMN, CAIRO... YOU'RE GOING ON A DIET.

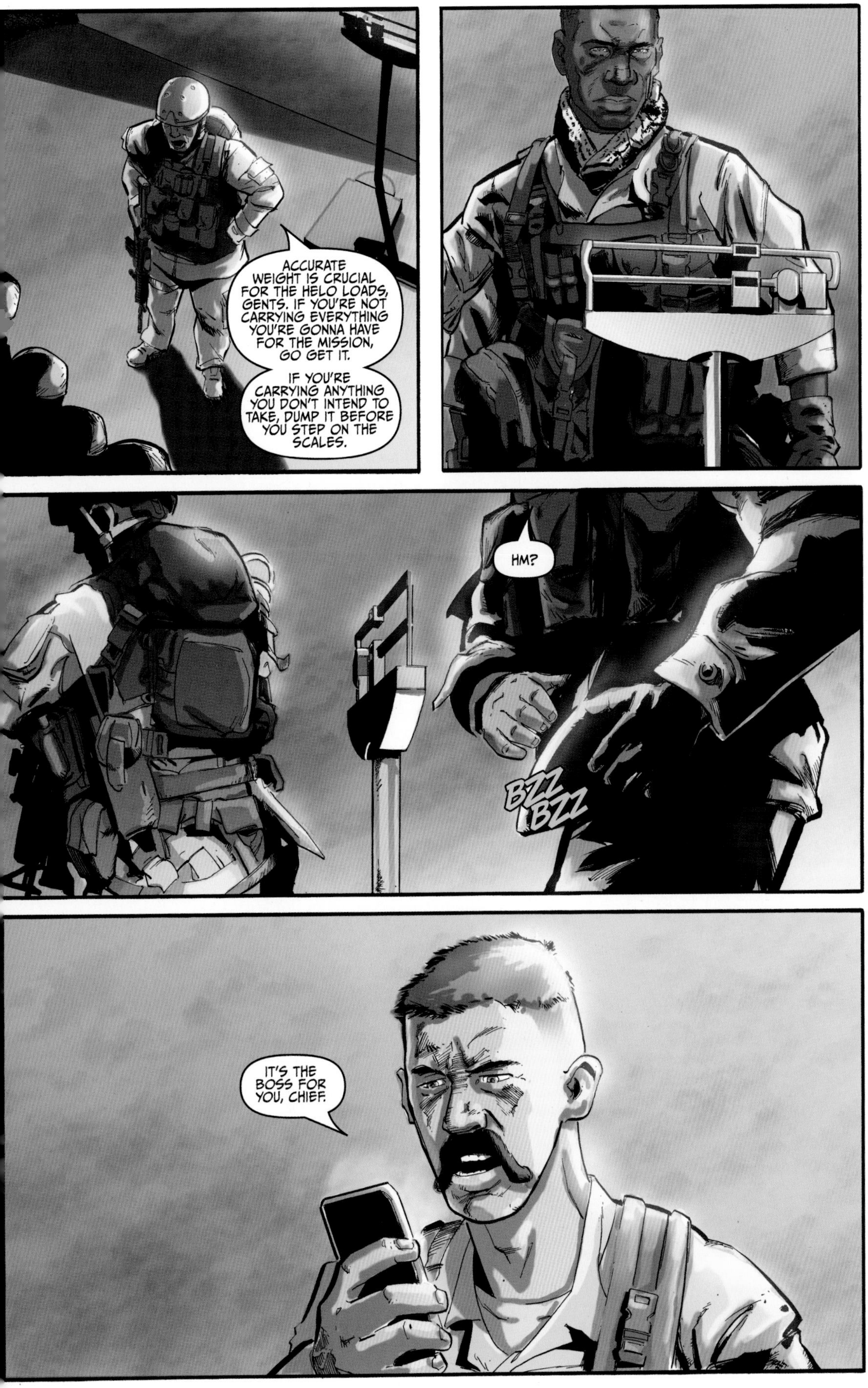
ACCURATE WEIGHT IS CRUCIAL FOR THE HELO LOADS, GENTS. IF YOU'RE NOT CARRYING EVERYTHING YOU'RE GONNA HAVE FOR THE MISSION, GO GET IT.
IF YOU'RE CARRYING ANYTHING YOU DON'T INTEND TO TAKE, DUMP IT BEFORE YOU STEP ON THE SCALES.
HM?
BZZ BZZ
IT'S THE BOSS FOR YOU, CHIEF.

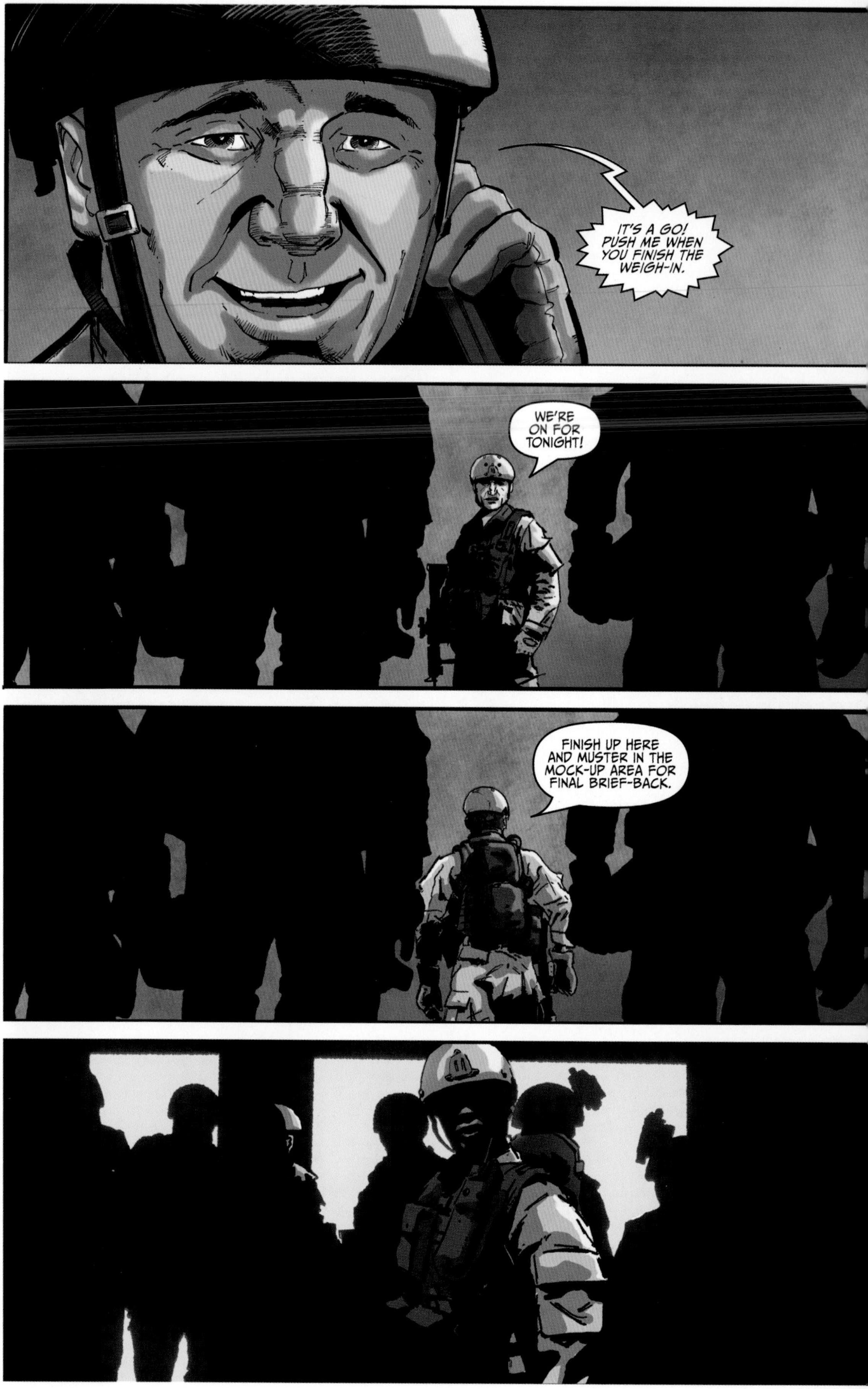
IT'S A GO! PUSH ME WHEN YOU FINISH THE WEIGH-IN.
WE'RE ON FOR TONIGHT!
FINISH UP HERE AND MUSTER IN THE MOCK-UP AREA FOR FINAL BRIEF-BACK.

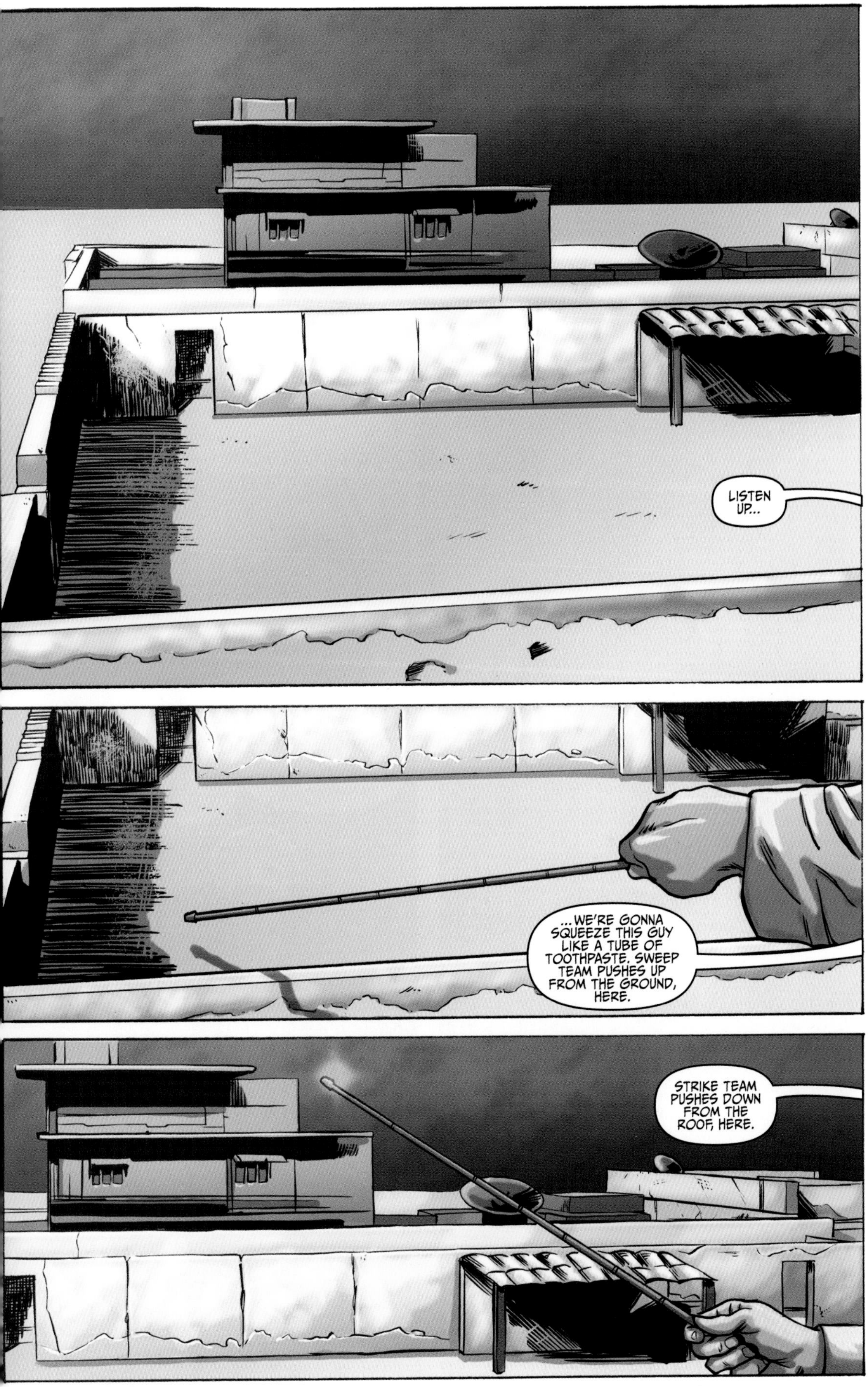
LISTEN UP...
...WE'RE GONNA SQUEEZE THIS GUY LIKE A TUBE OF TOOTHPASTE. SWEEP TEAM PUSHES UP FROM THE GROUND, HERE.
STRIKE TEAM PUSHES DOWN FROM THE ROOF, HERE.

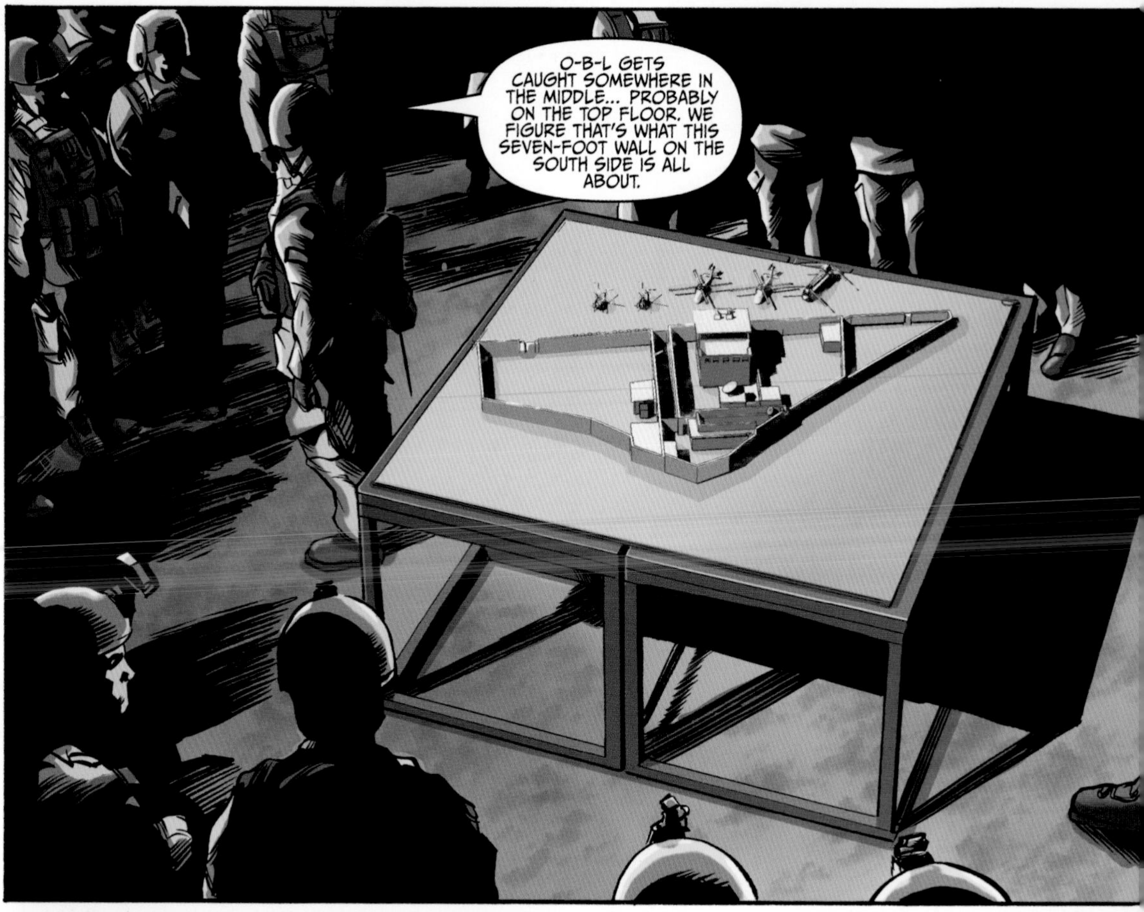
O-B-L GETS CAUGHT SOMEWHERE IN THE MIDDLE... PROBABLY ON THE TOP FLOOR. WE FIGURE THAT'S WHAT THIS SEVEN-FOOT WALL ON THE SOUTH SIDE IS ALL ABOUT.

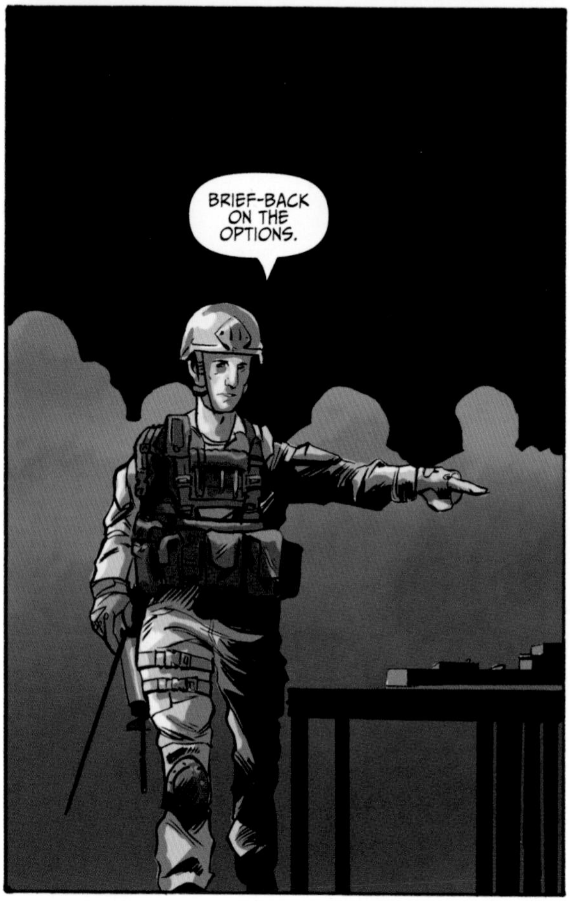
BRIEF-BACK ON THE OPTIONS.

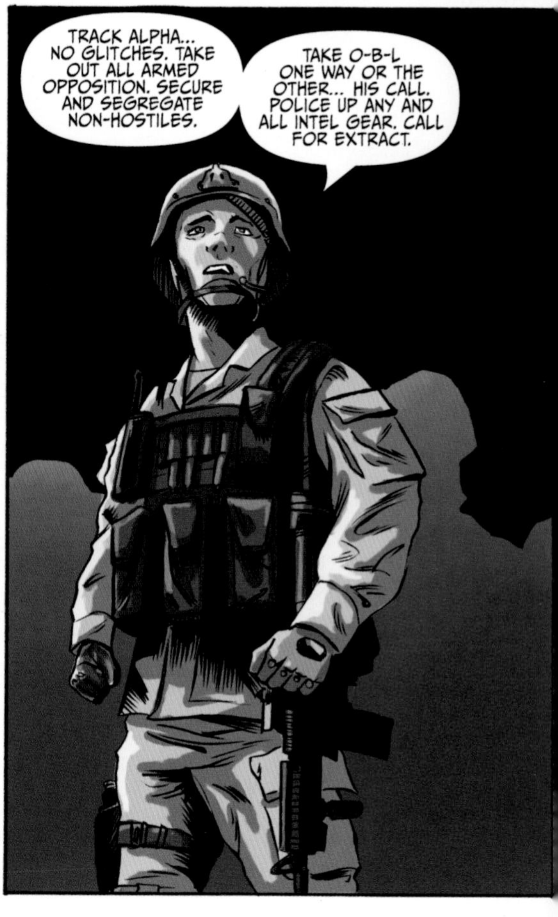
TRACK ALPHA... NO GLITCHES. TAKE OUT ALL ARMED OPPOSITION. SECURE AND SEGREGATE NON-HOSTILES.
TAKE O-B-L ONE WAY OR THE OTHER... HIS CALL. POLICE UP ANY AND ALL INTEL GEAR. CALL FOR EXTRACT.

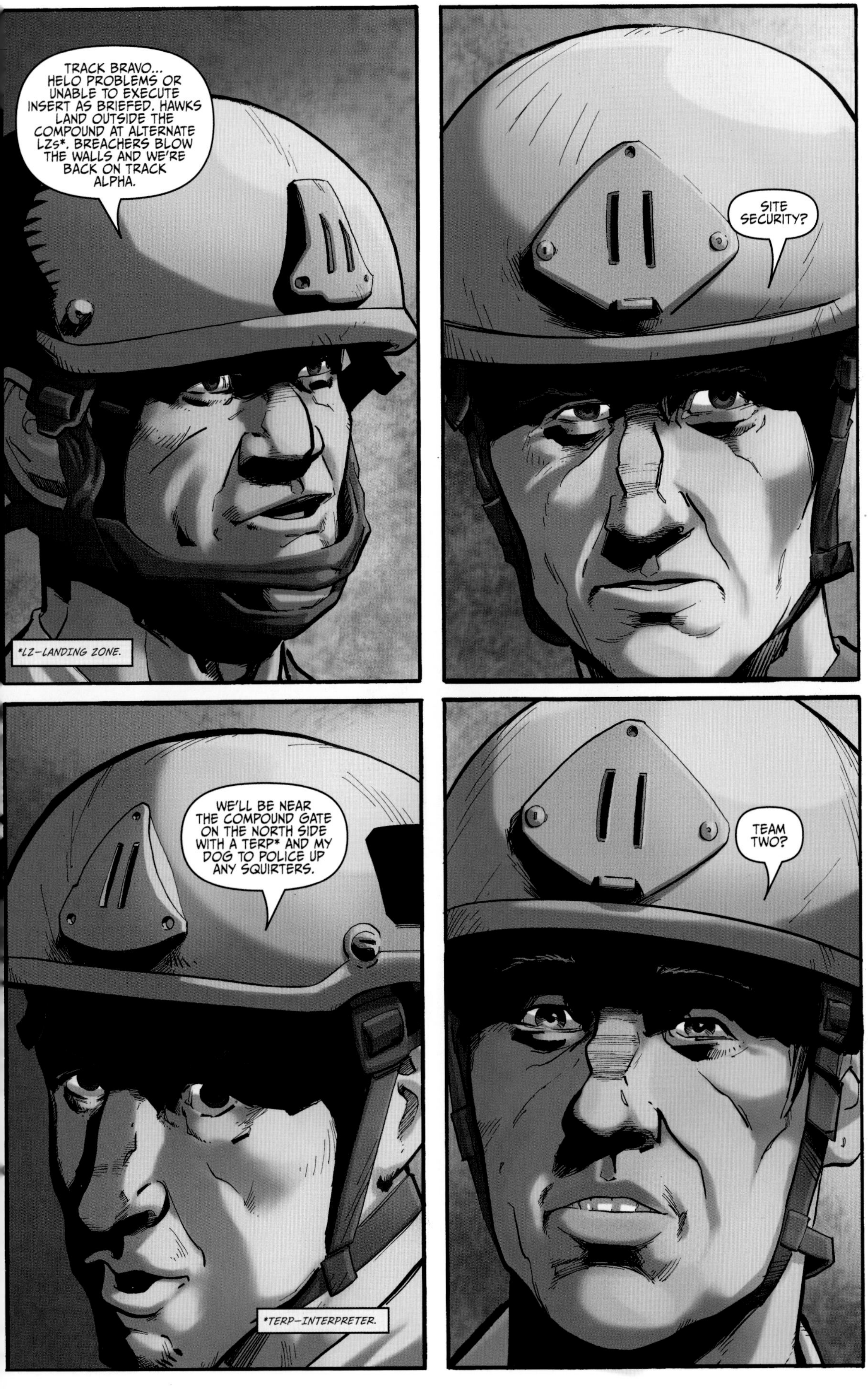
TRACK BRAVO... HELO PROBLEMS OR UNABLE TO EXECUTE INSERT AS BRIEFED. HAWKS LAND OUTSIDE THE COMPOUND AT ALTERNATE LZs*. BREACHERS BLOW THE WALLS AND WE'RE BACK ON TRACK ALPHA.
*LZ—LANDING ZONE.
SITE SECURITY?
WE'LL BE NEAR THE COMPOUND GATE ON THE NORTH SIDE WITH A TERP* AND MY DOG TO POLICE UP ANY SQUIRTERS.
*TERP—INTERPRETER.
TEAM TWO?

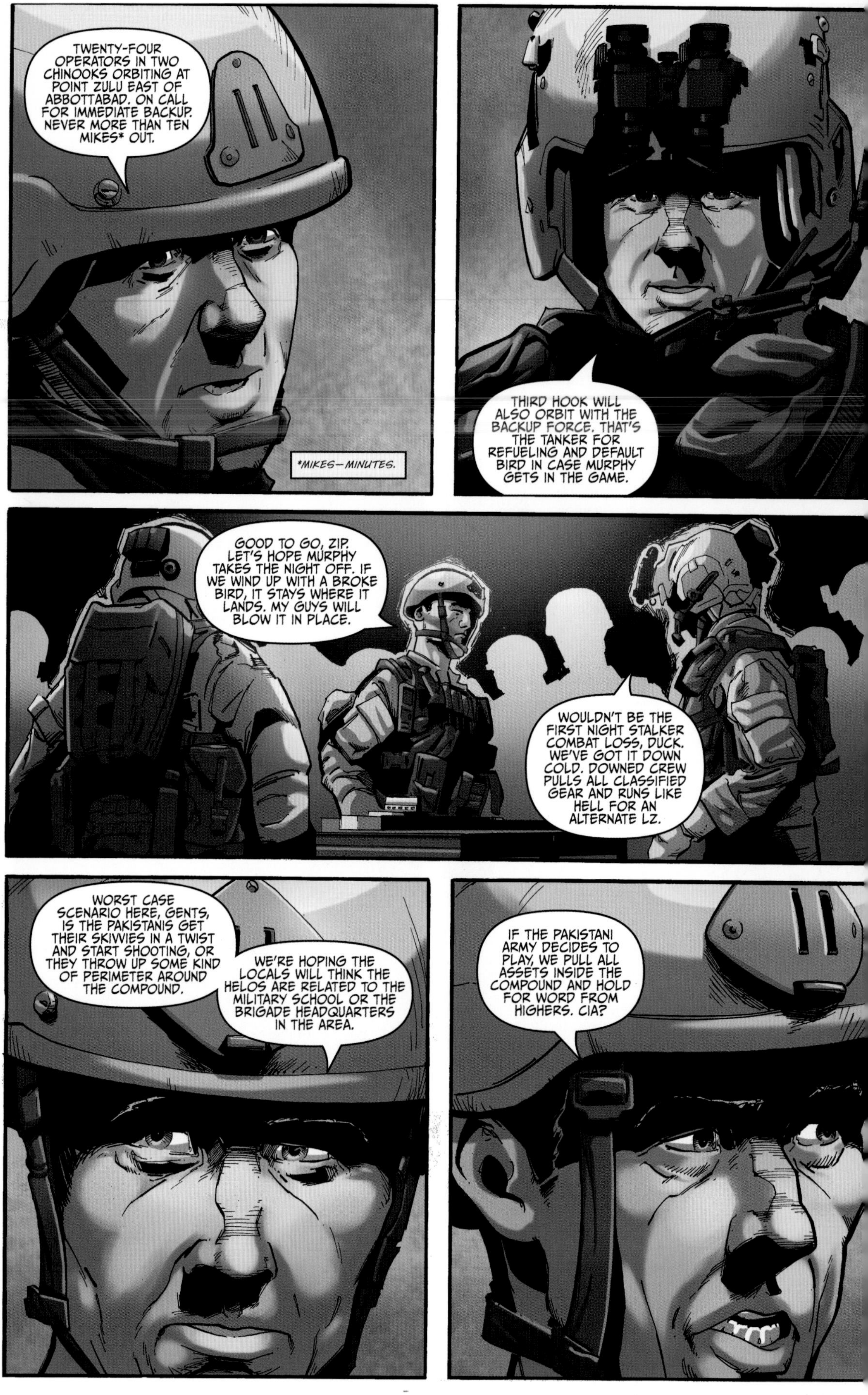
TWENTY-FOUR OPERATORS IN TWO CHINOOKS ORBITING AT POINT ZULU EAST OF ABBOTTABAD. ON CALL FOR IMMEDIATE BACKUP. NEVER MORE THAN TEN MIKES* OUT.
*MIKES—MINUTES.
THIRD HOOK WILL ALSO ORBIT WITH THE BACKUP FORCE. THAT'S THE TANKER FOR REFUELING AND DEFAULT BIRD IN CASE MURPHY GETS IN THE GAME.
GOOD TO GO, ZIP. LET'S HOPE MURPHY TAKES THE NIGHT OFF. IF WE WIND UP WITH A BROKE BIRD, IT STAYS WHERE IT LANDS. MY GUYS WILL BLOW IT IN PLACE.
WOULDN'T BE THE FIRST NIGHT STALKER COMBAT LOSS, DUCK. WE'VE GOT IT DOWN COLD. DOWNED CREW PULLS ALL CLASSIFIED GEAR AND RUNS LIKE HELL FOR AN ALTERNATE LZ.
WORST CASE SCENARIO HERE, GENTS, IS THE PAKISTANIS GET THEIR SKIVVIES IN A TWIST AND START SHOOTING, OR THEY THROW UP SOME KIND OF PERIMETER AROUND THE COMPOUND.
WE'RE HOPING THE LOCALS WILL THINK THE HELOS ARE RELATED TO THE MILITARY SCHOOL OR THE BRIGADE HEADQUARTERS IN THE AREA.
IF THE PAKISTANI ARMY DECIDES TO PLAY, WE PULL ALL ASSETS INSIDE THE COMPOUND AND HOLD FOR WORD FROM HIGHERS. CIA?

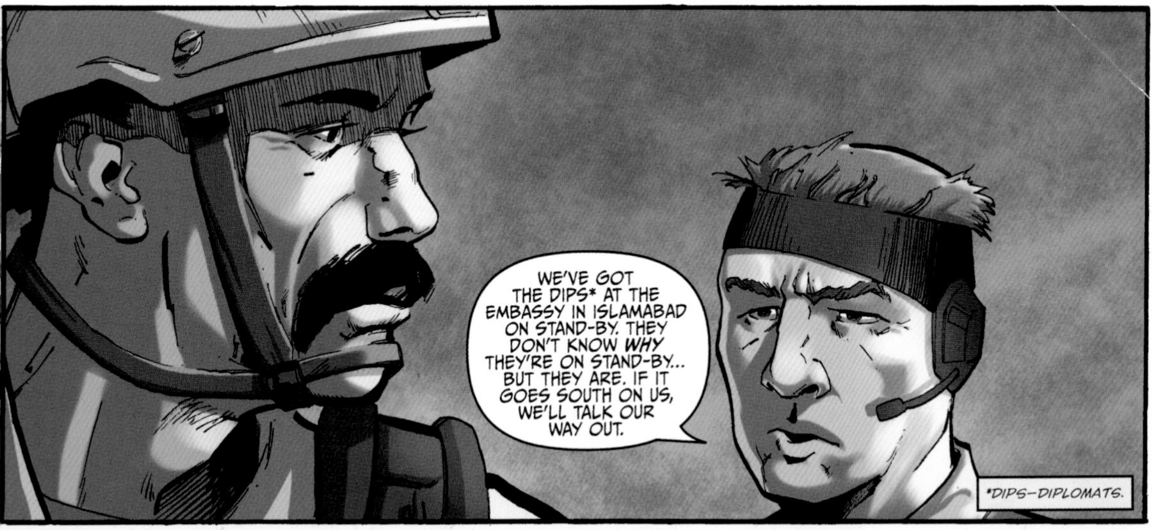
WE'VE GOT THE DIPS* AT THE EMBASSY IN ISLAMABAD ON STAND-BY. THEY DON'T KNOW *WHY* THEY'RE ON STAND-BY... BUT THEY ARE. IF IT GOES SOUTH ON US, WE'LL TALK OUR WAY OUT.
*DIPS—DIPLOMATS.

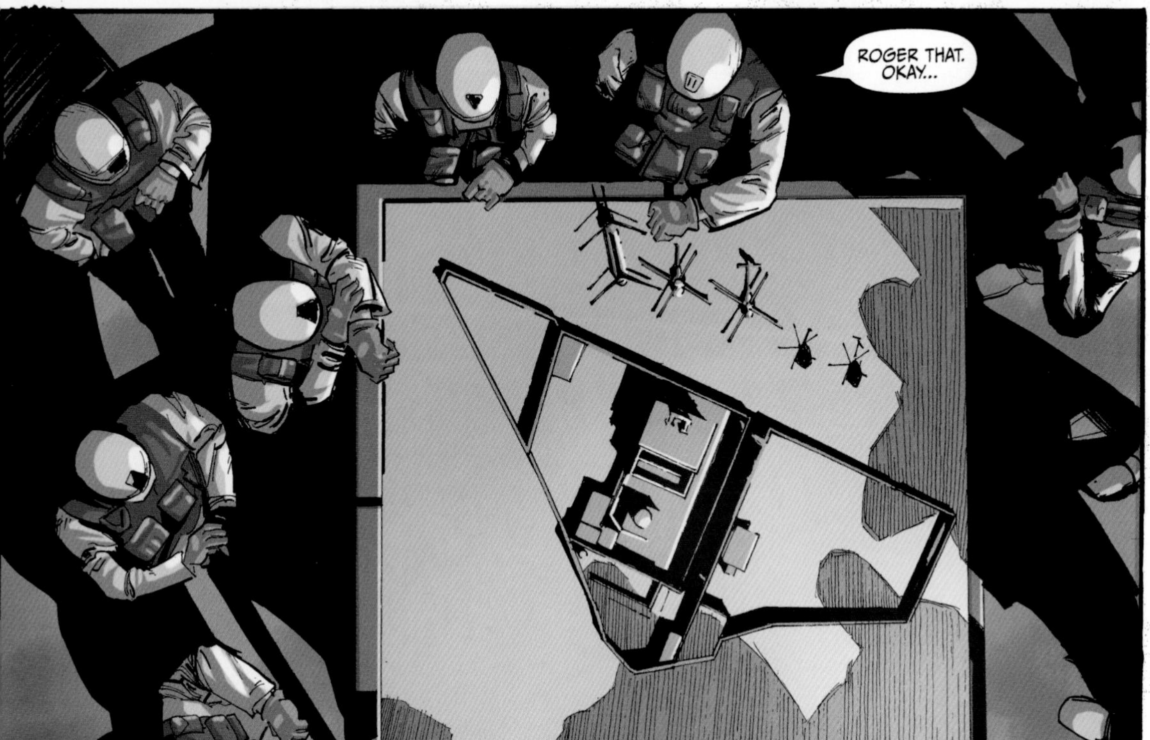
ROGER THAT. OKAY...

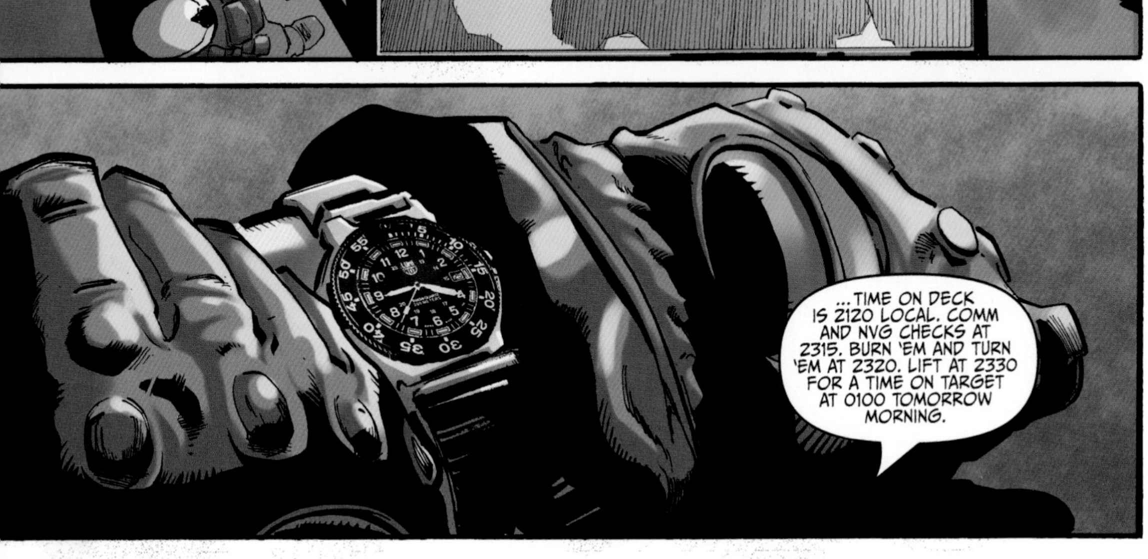
...TIME ON DECK IS 2120 LOCAL. COMM AND NVG CHECKS AT 2315. BURN 'EM AND TURN 'EM AT 2320. LIFT AT 2330 FOR A TIME ON TARGET AT 0100 TOMORROW MORNING.

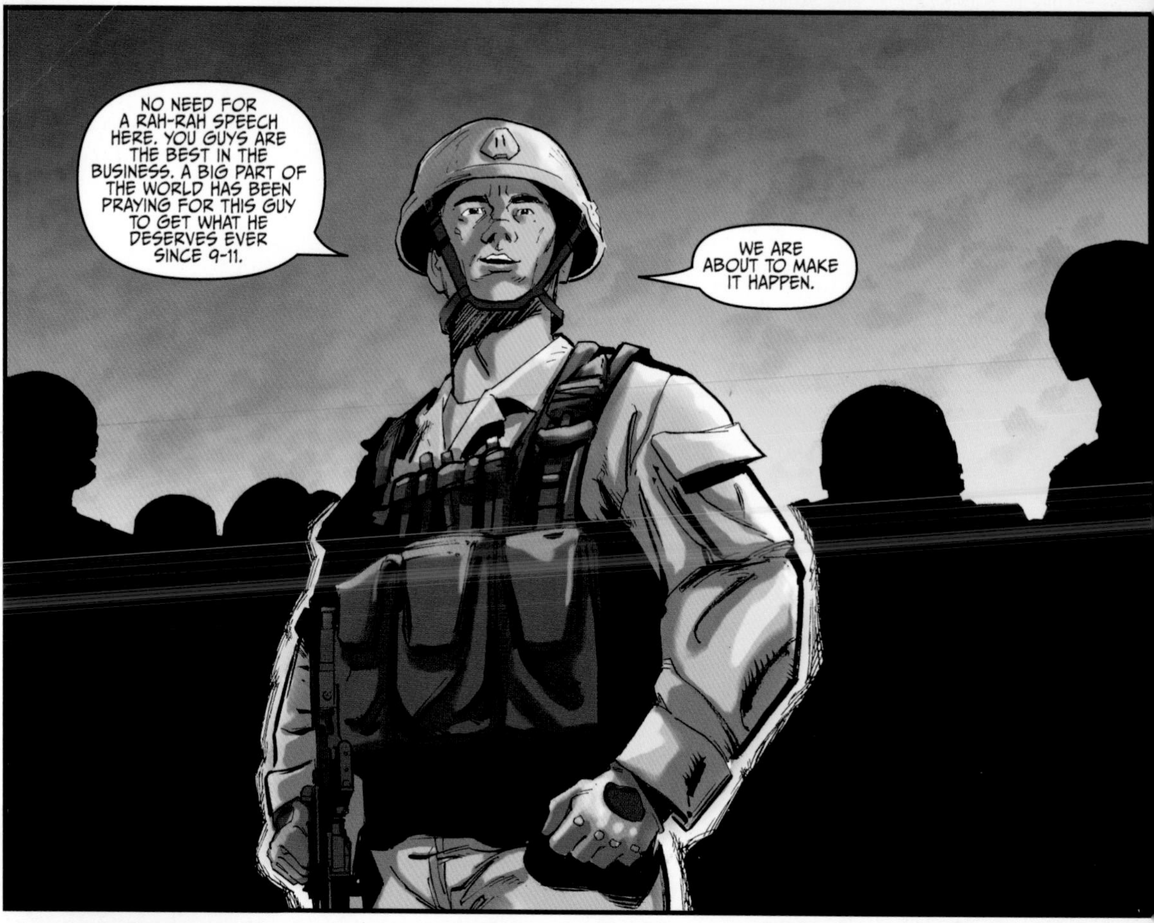
NO NEED FOR A RAH-RAH SPEECH HERE. YOU GUYS ARE THE BEST IN THE BUSINESS. A BIG PART OF THE WORLD HAS BEEN PRAYING FOR THIS GUY TO GET WHAT HE DESERVES EVER SINCE 9-11.
WE ARE ABOUT TO MAKE IT HAPPEN.

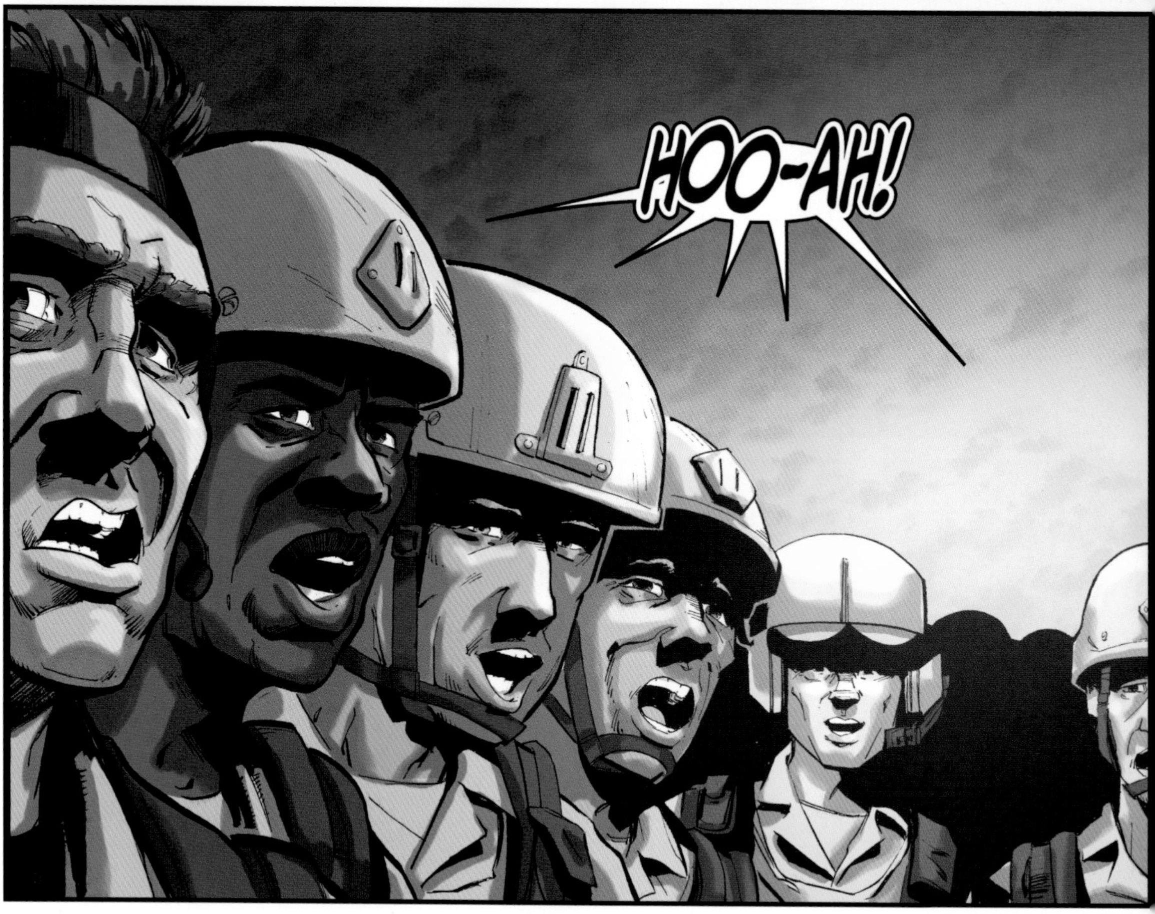
HOO-AH!

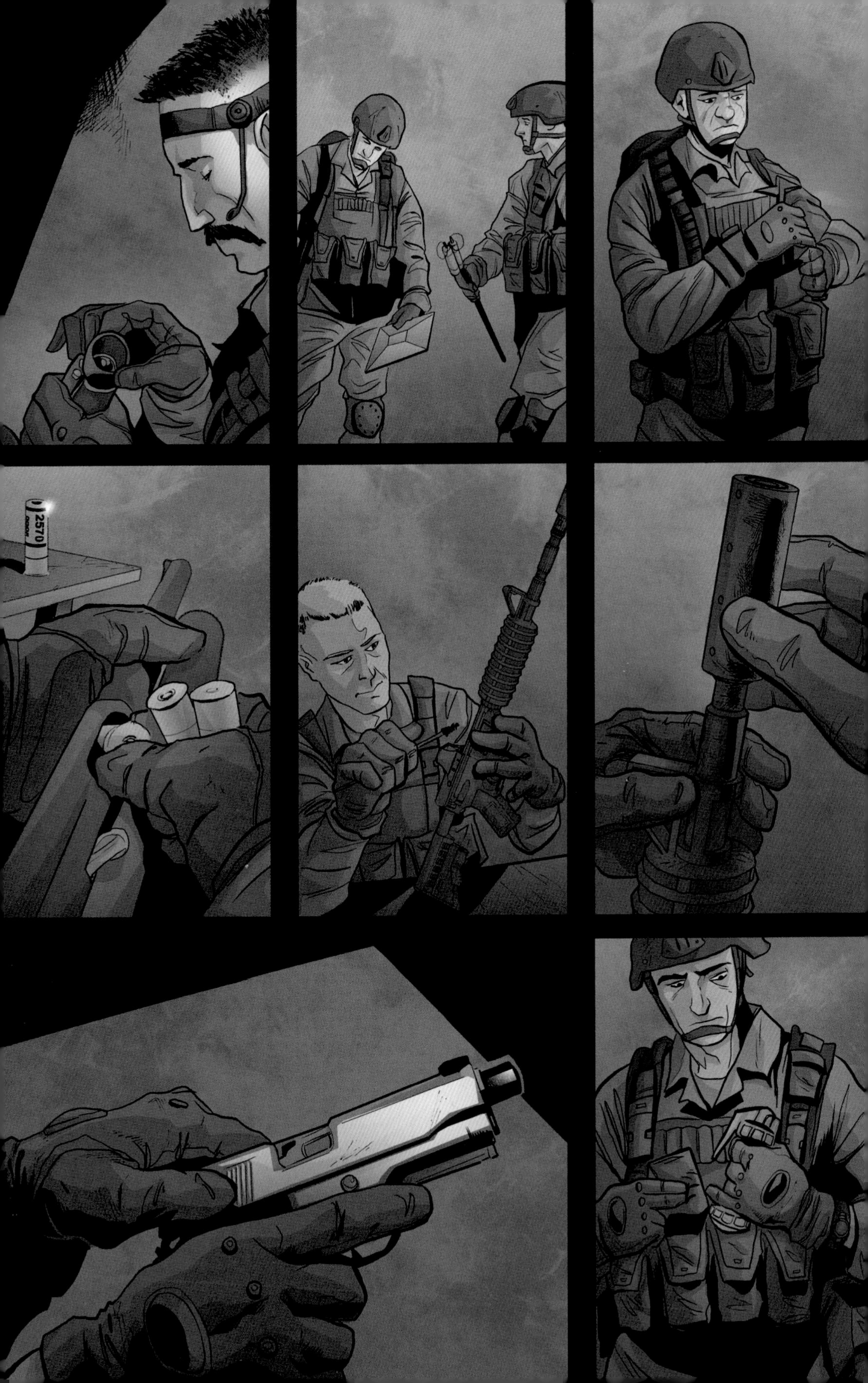
2570

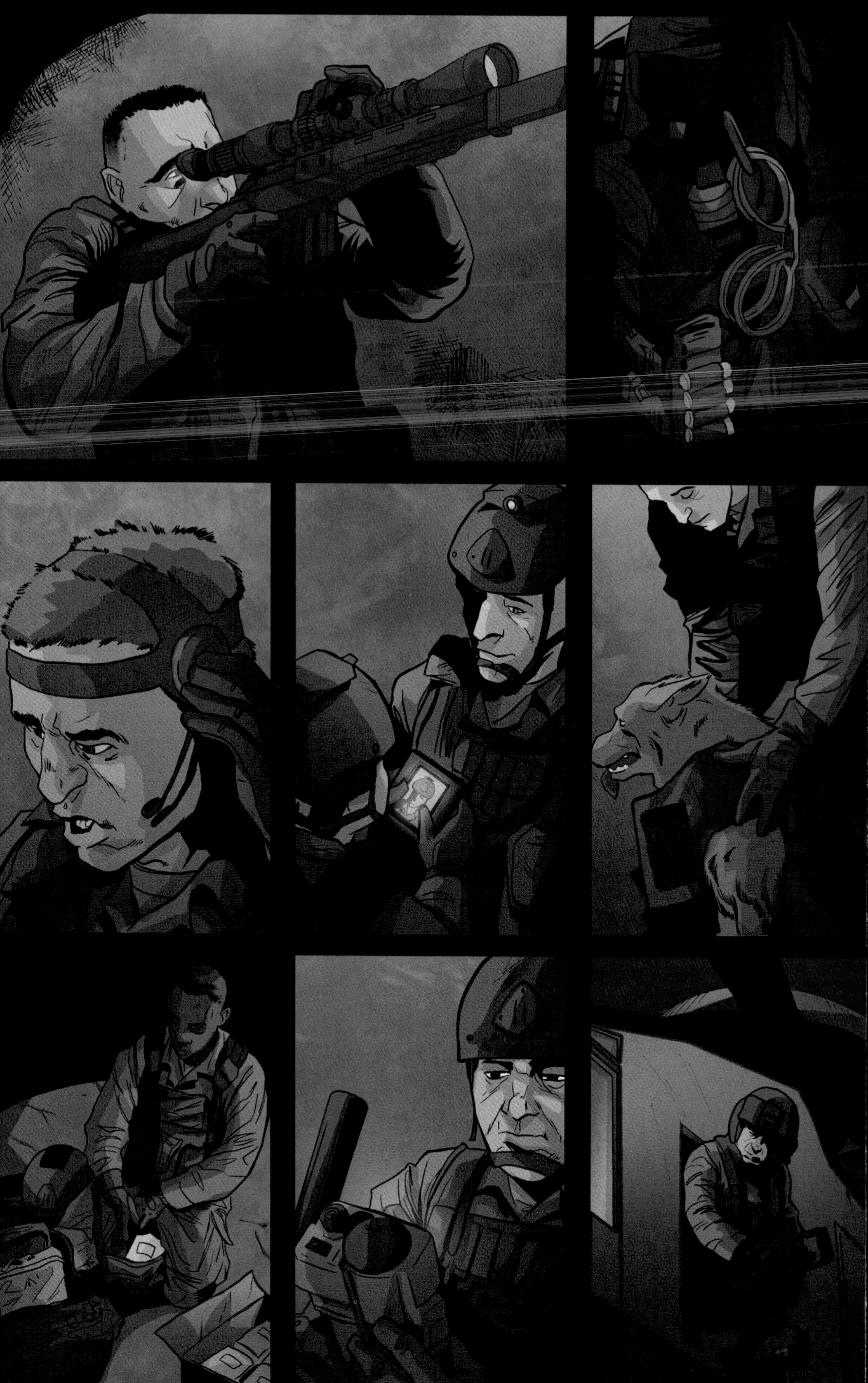

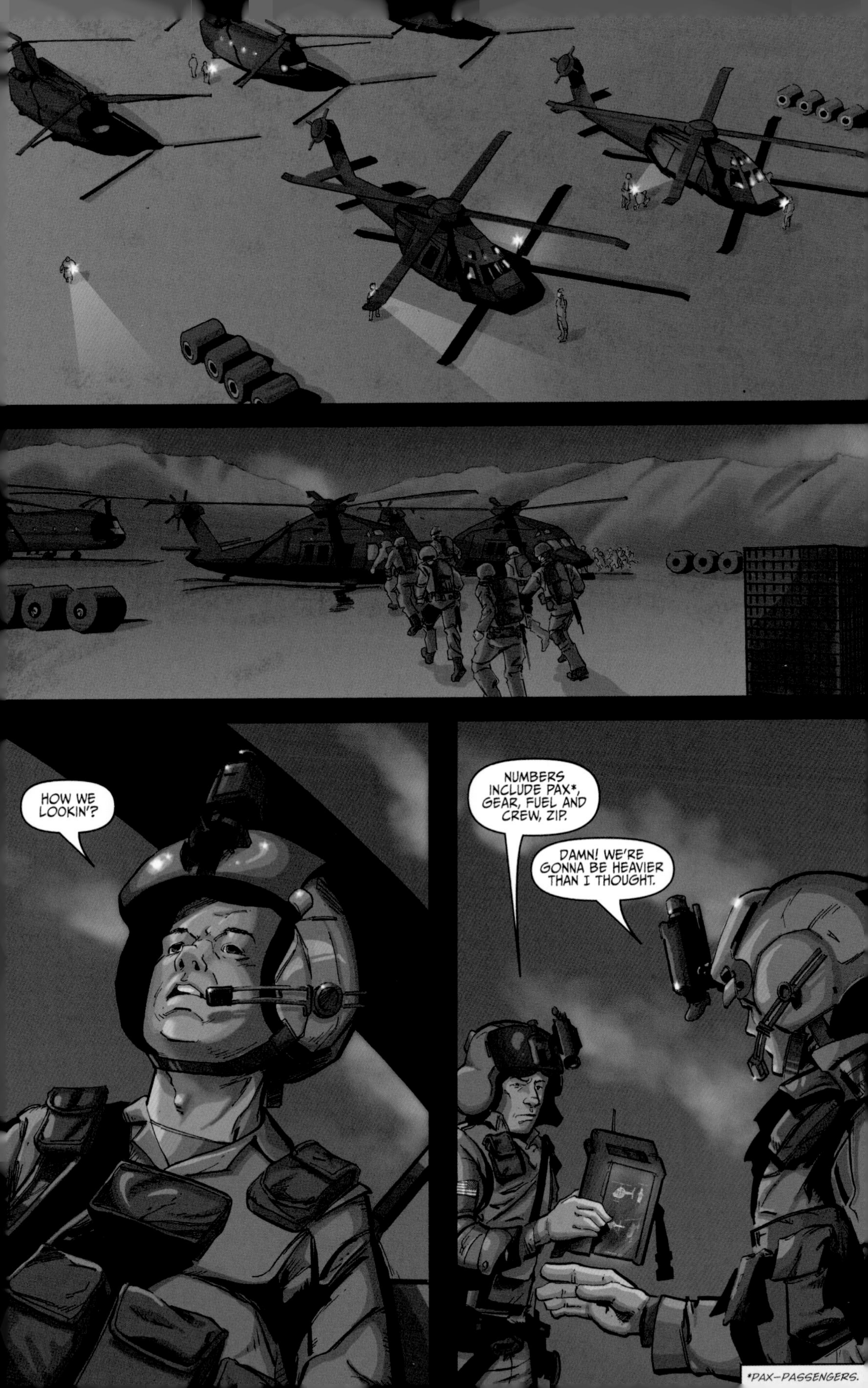
HOW WE LOOKIN'?
NUMBERS INCLUDE PAX*, GEAR, FUEL AND CREW, ZIP.
DAMN! WE'RE GONNA BE HEAVIER THAN I THOUGHT.
*PAX—PASSENGERS.

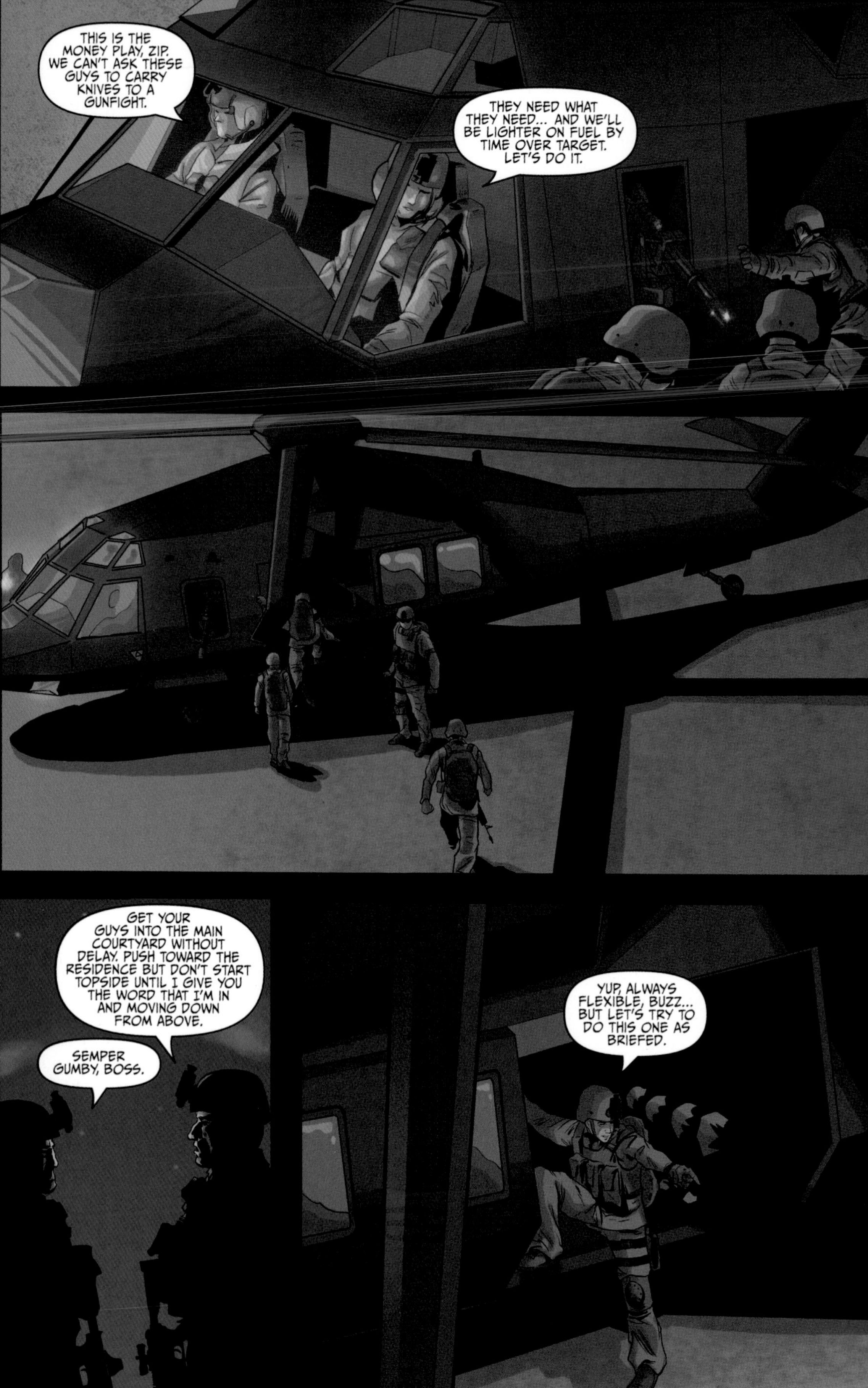
THIS IS THE MONEY PLAY, ZIP. WE CAN'T ASK THESE GUYS TO CARRY KNIVES TO A GUNFIGHT.
THEY NEED WHAT THEY NEED... AND WE'LL BE LIGHTER ON FUEL BY TIME OVER TARGET. LET'S DO IT.
GET YOUR GUYS INTO THE MAIN COURTYARD WITHOUT DELAY. PUSH TOWARD THE RESIDENCE BUT DON'T START TOPSIDE UNTIL I GIVE YOU THE WORD THAT I'M IN AND MOVING DOWN FROM ABOVE.
SEMPER GUMBY, BOSS.
YUP, ALWAYS FLEXIBLE, BUZZ... BUT LET'S TRY TO DO THIS ONE AS BRIEFED.

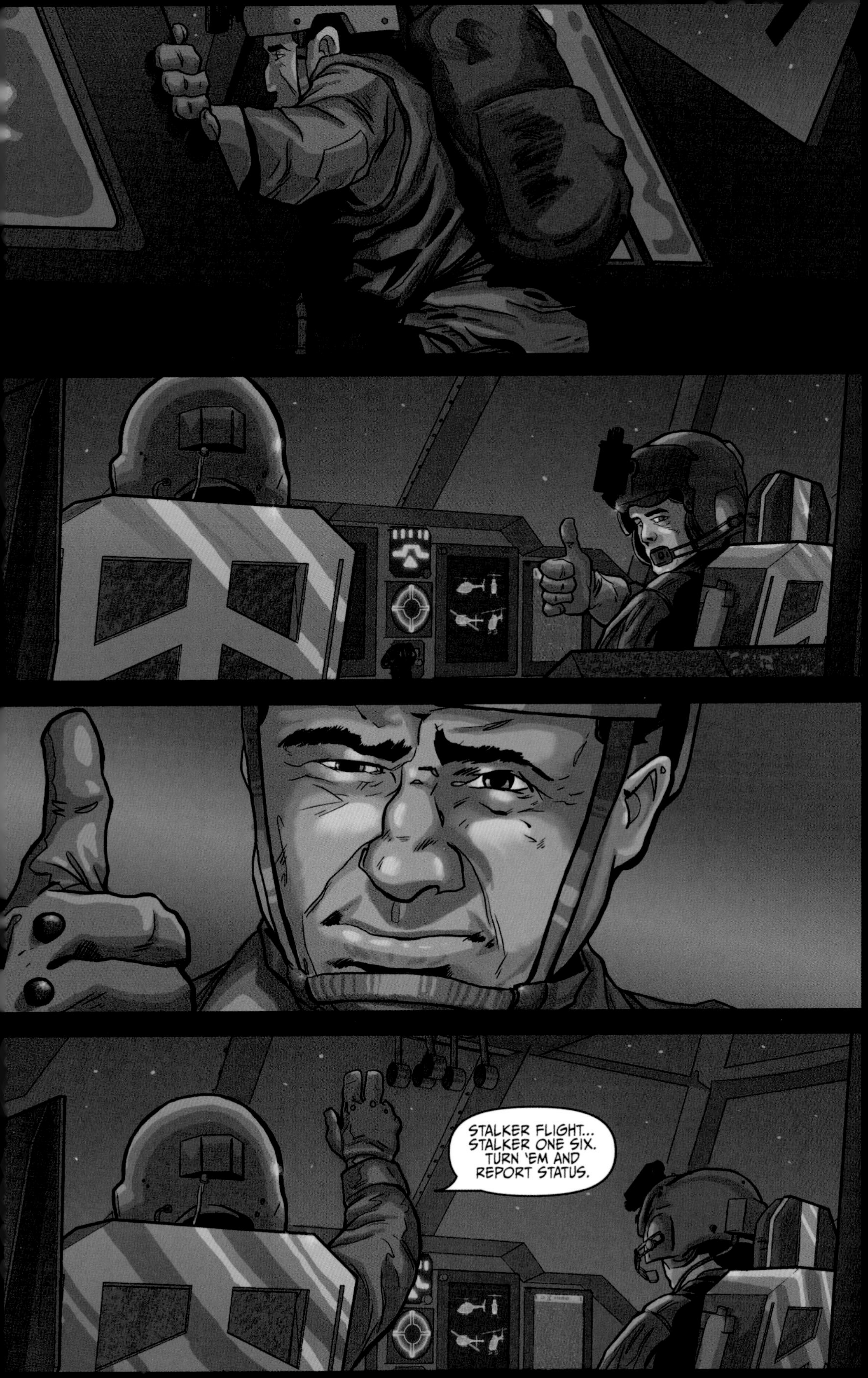
STALKER FLIGHT... STALKER ONE SIX. TURN 'EM AND REPORT STATUS.

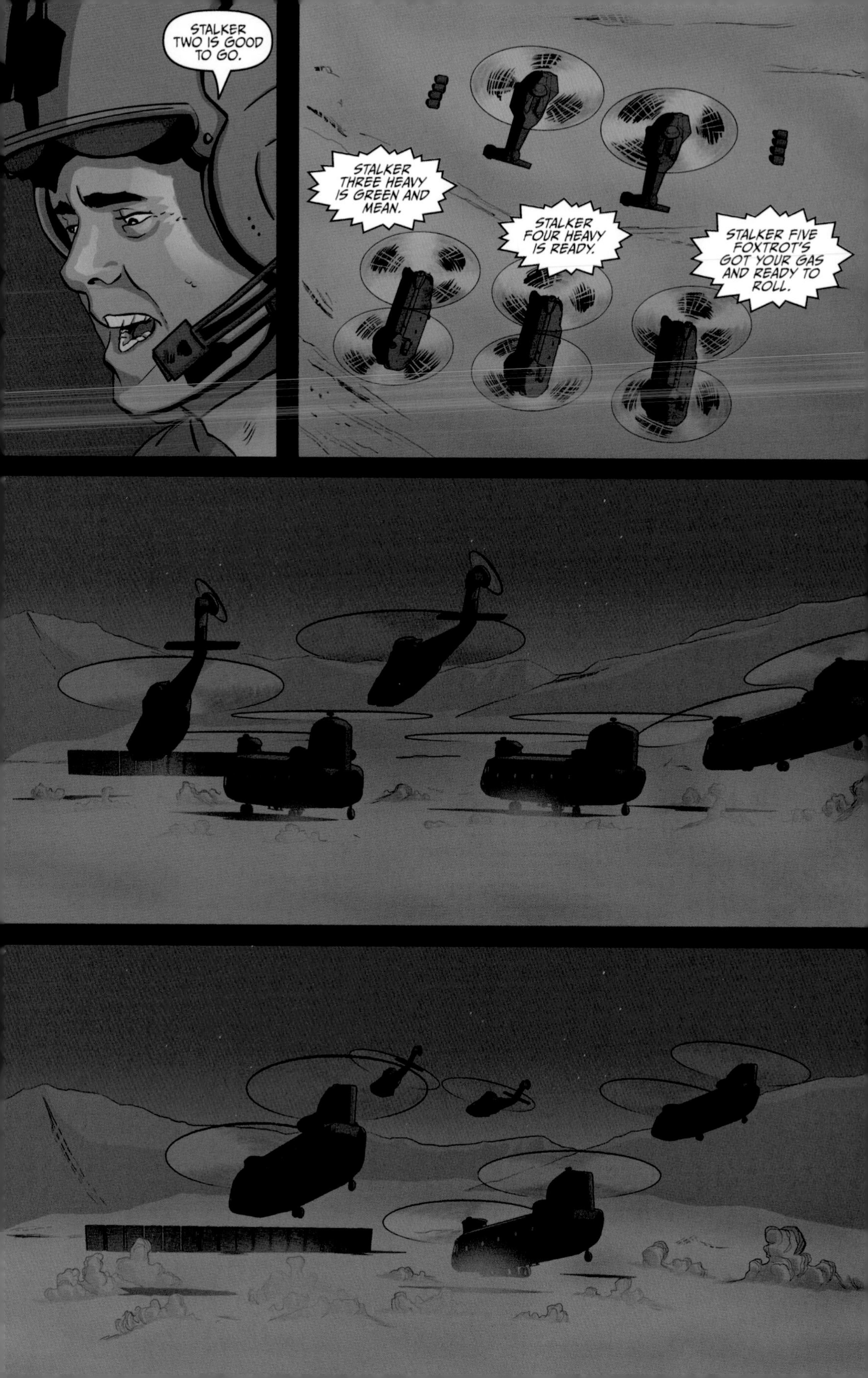
STALKER TWO IS GOOD TO GO.
STALKER THREE HEAVY IS GREEN AND MEAN.
STALKER FOUR HEAVY IS READY.
STALKER FIVE FOXTROT'S GOT YOUR GAS AND READY TO ROLL.

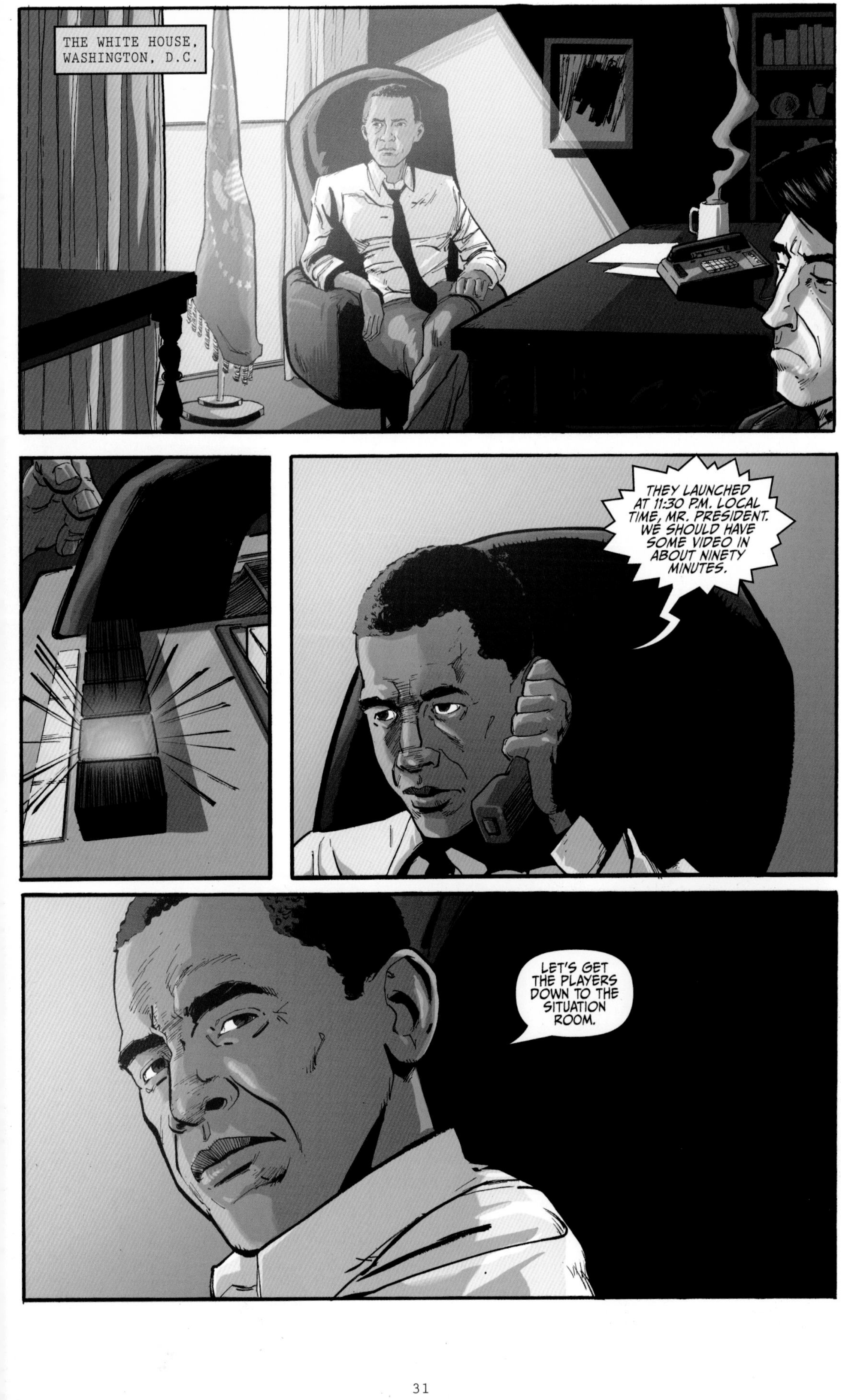
THE WHITE HOUSE, WASHINGTON, D.C.
THEY LAUNCHED AT 11:30 P.M. LOCAL TIME, MR. PRESIDENT. WE SHOULD HAVE SOME VIDEO IN ABOUT NINETY MINUTES.
LET'S GET THE PLAYERS DOWN TO THE SITUATION ROOM.

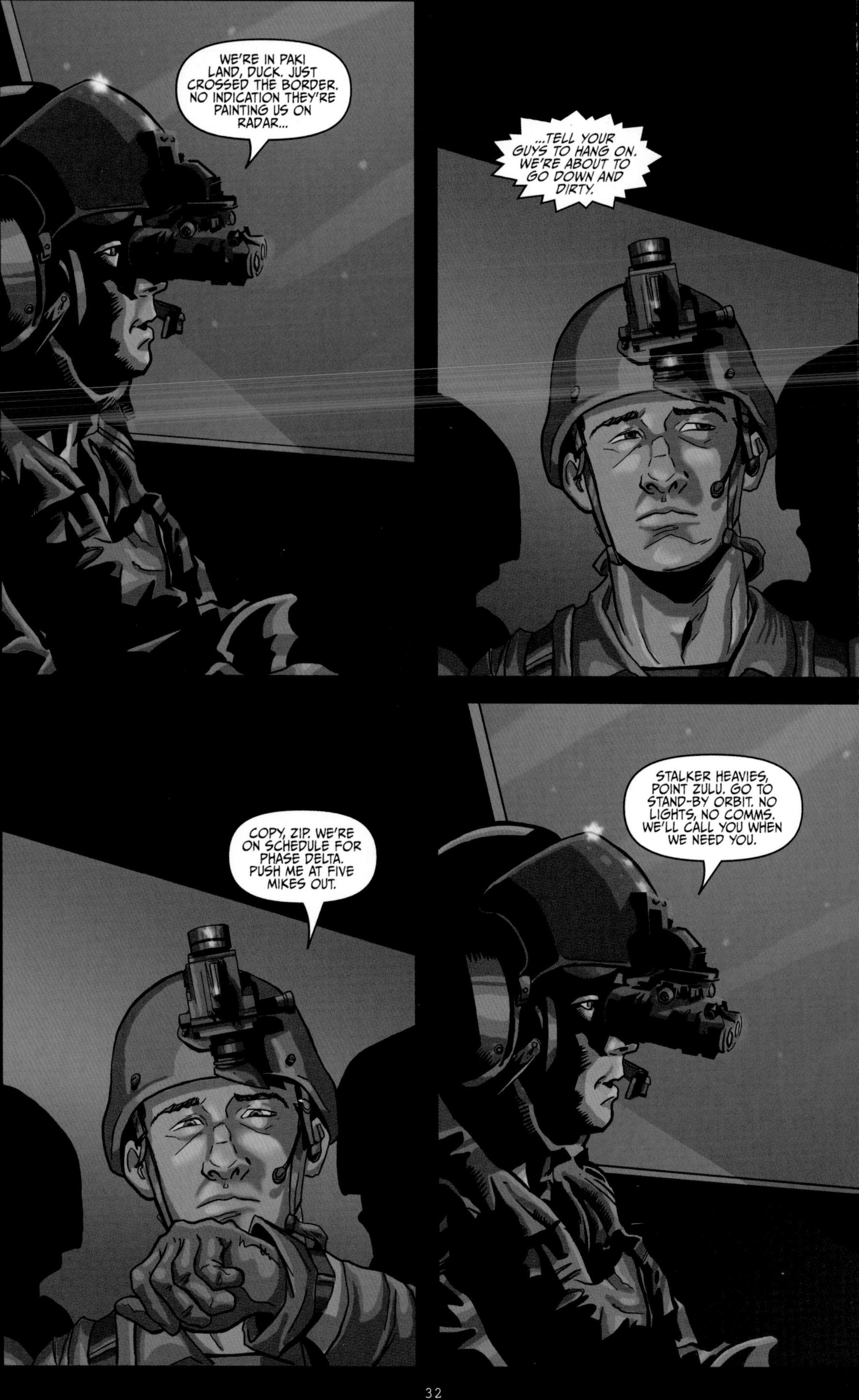
WE'RE IN PAKI LAND, DUCK. JUST CROSSED THE BORDER. NO INDICATION THEY'RE PAINTING US ON RADAR...
...TELL YOUR GUYS TO HANG ON. WE'RE ABOUT TO GO DOWN AND DIRTY.
COPY, ZIP. WE'RE ON SCHEDULE FOR PHASE DELTA. PUSH ME AT FIVE MIKES OUT.
STALKER HEAVIES, POINT ZULU. GO TO STAND-BY ORBIT. NO LIGHTS, NO COMMS. WE'LL CALL YOU WHEN WE NEED YOU.

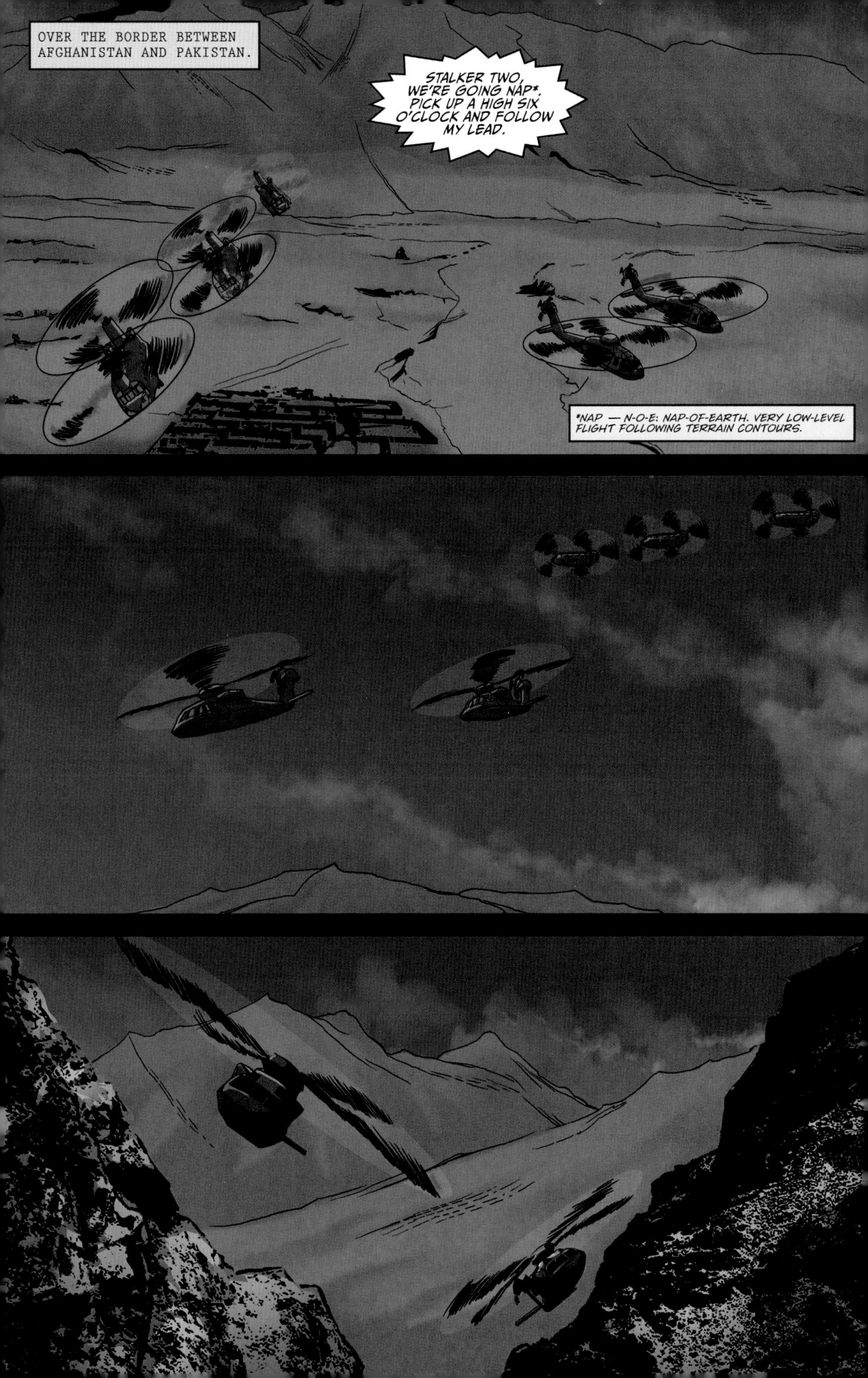
OVER THE BORDER BETWEEN AFGHANISTAN AND PAKISTAN.
STALKER TWO, WE'RE GOING NAP*. PICK UP A HIGH SIX O'CLOCK AND FOLLOW MY LEAD.
*NAP — N-O-E: NAP-OF-EARTH. VERY LOW-LEVEL FLIGHT FOLLOWING TERRAIN CONTOURS.

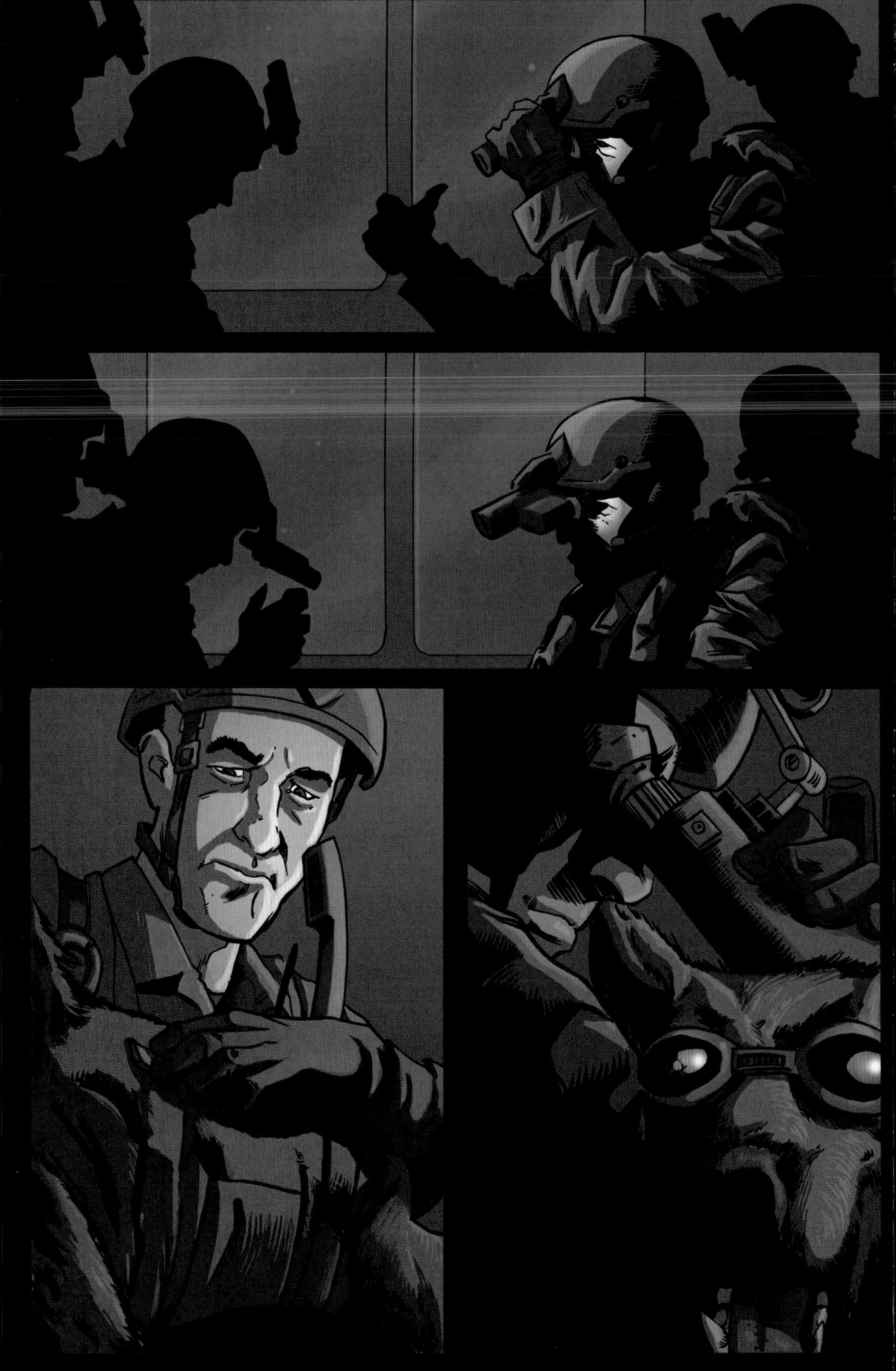

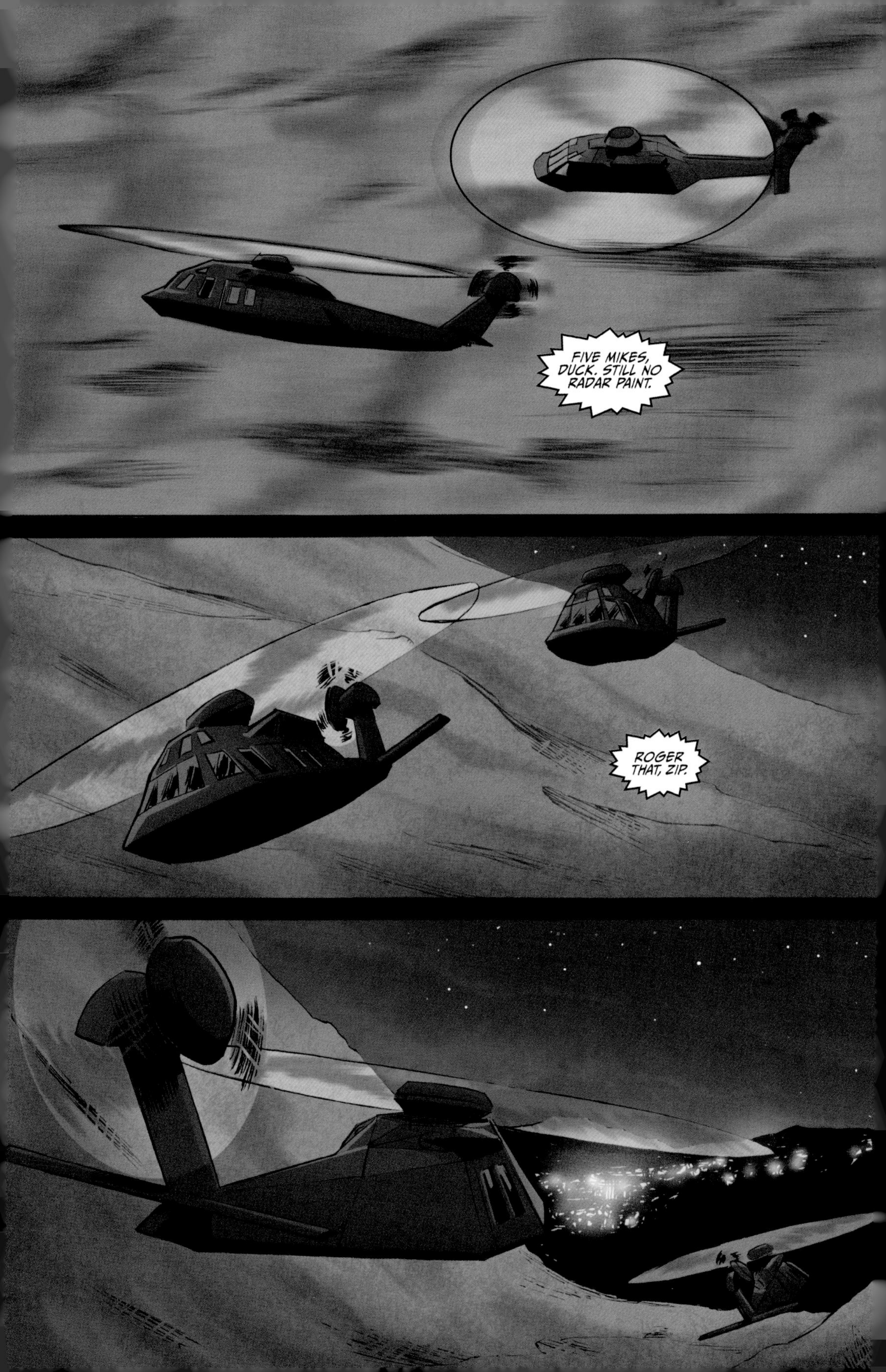
FIVE MIKES, DUCK. STILL NO RADAR PAINT.
ROGER THAT, ZIP.

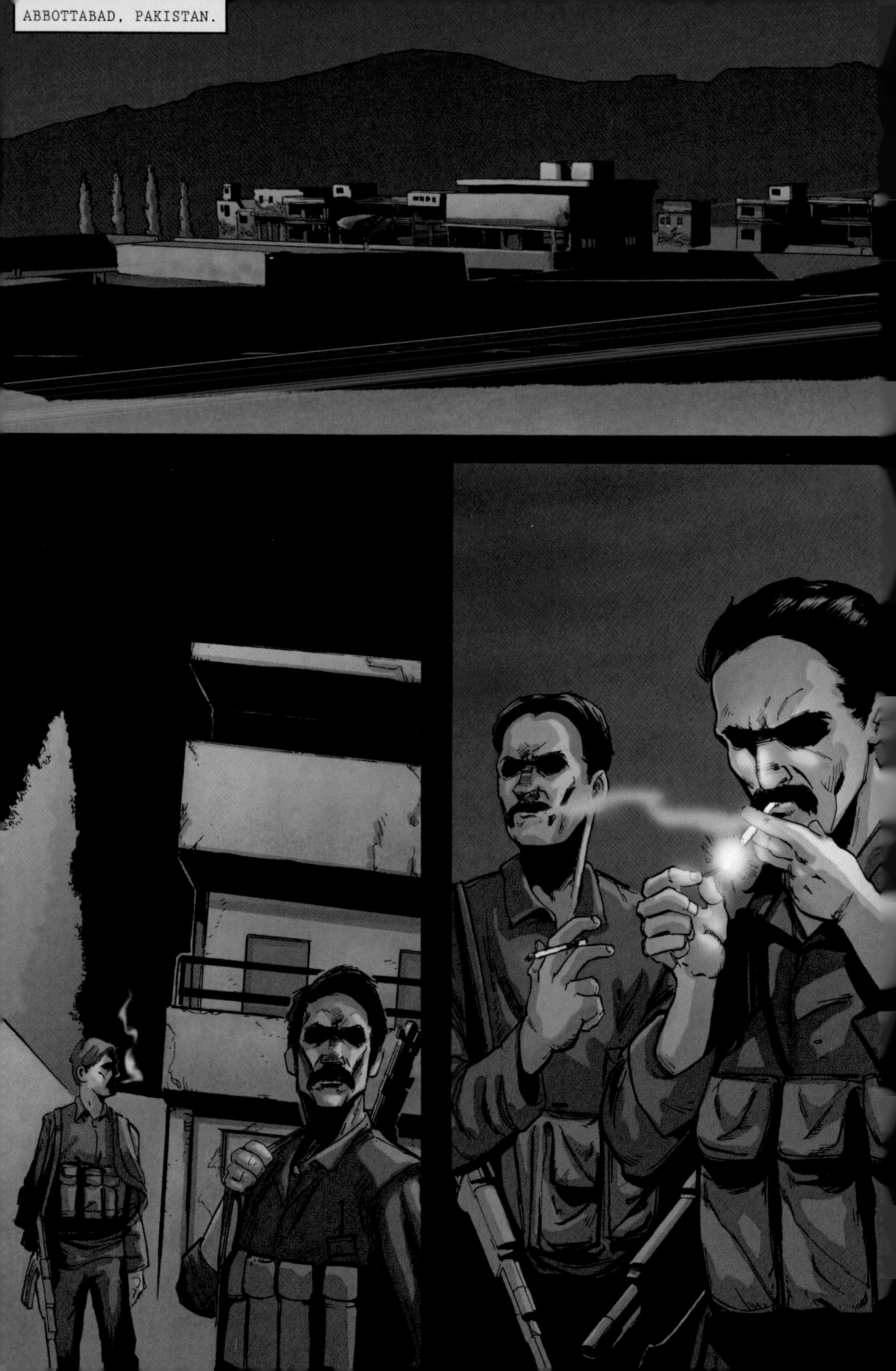
ABBOTTABAD, PAKISTAN.

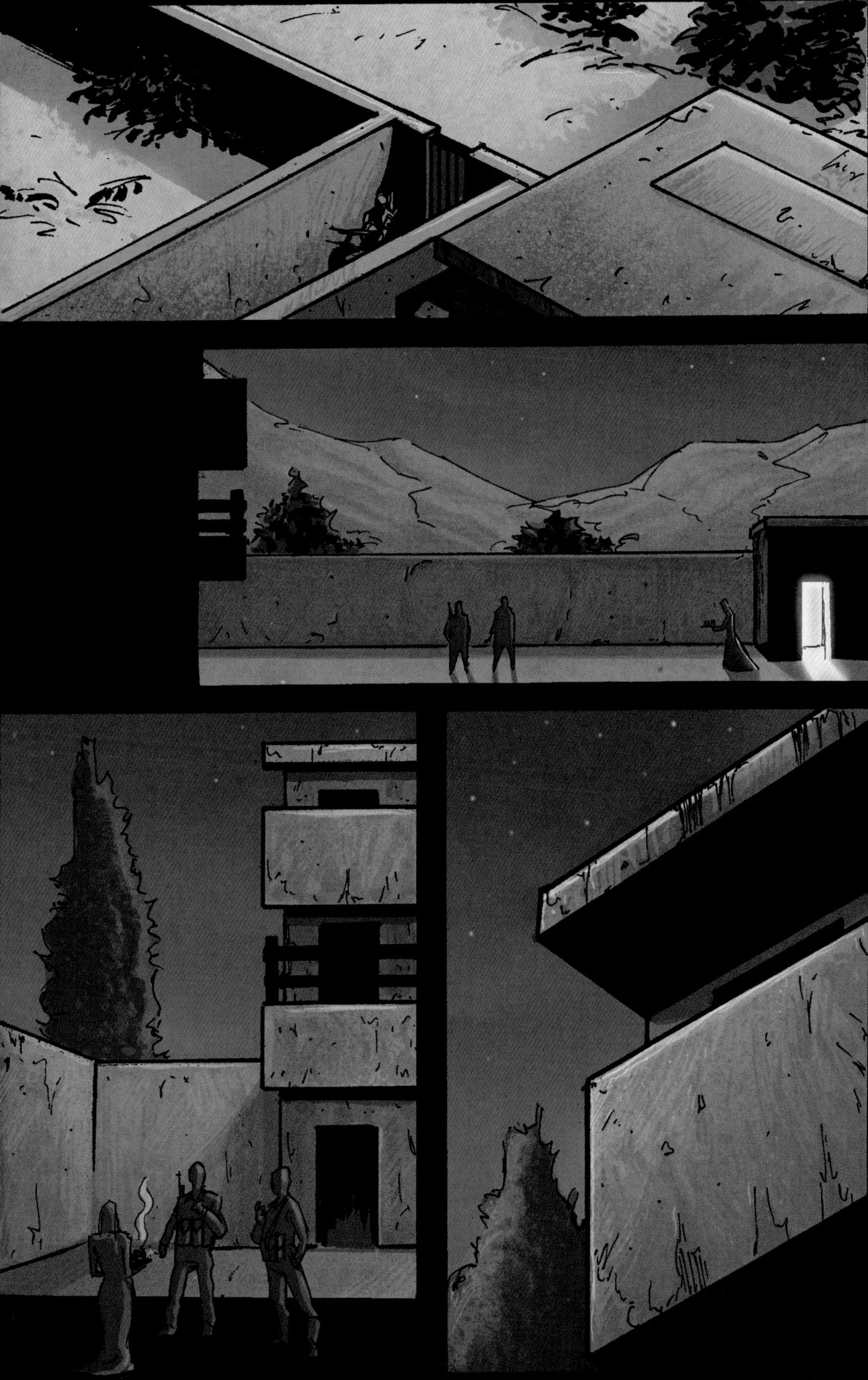

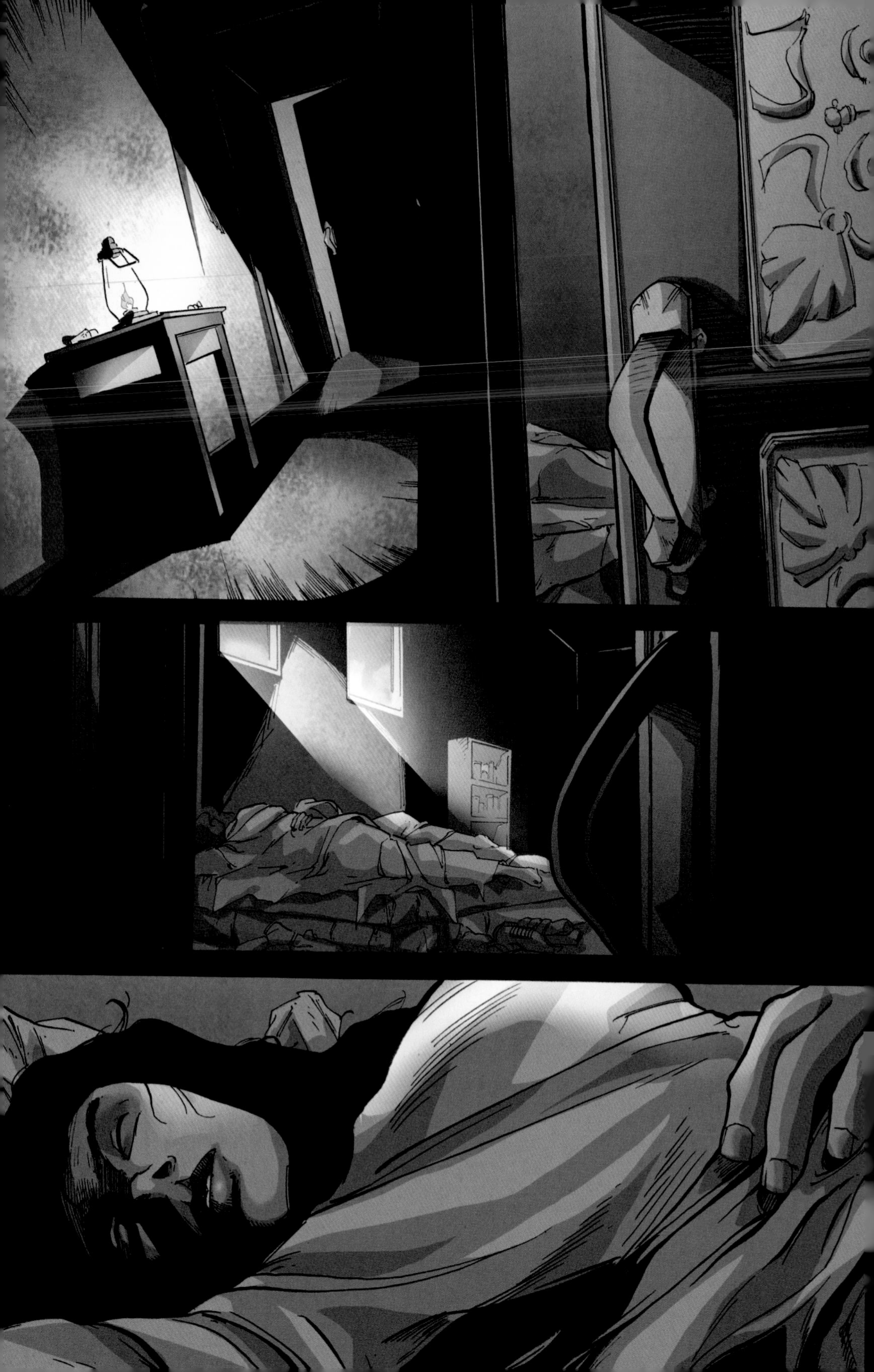

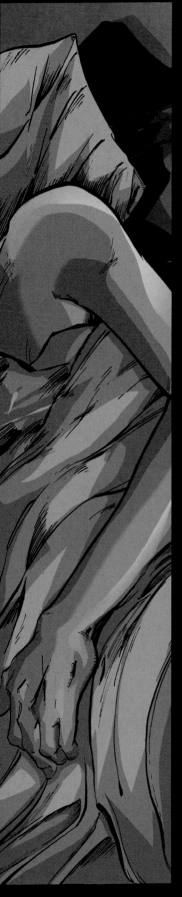

OSAMA BIN LADEN.
LEADER, AL-QAEDA.
INTERNATIONAL
TERRORIST.

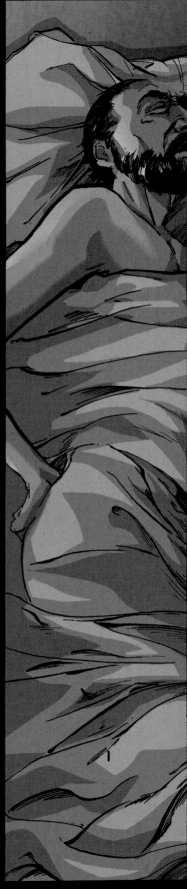

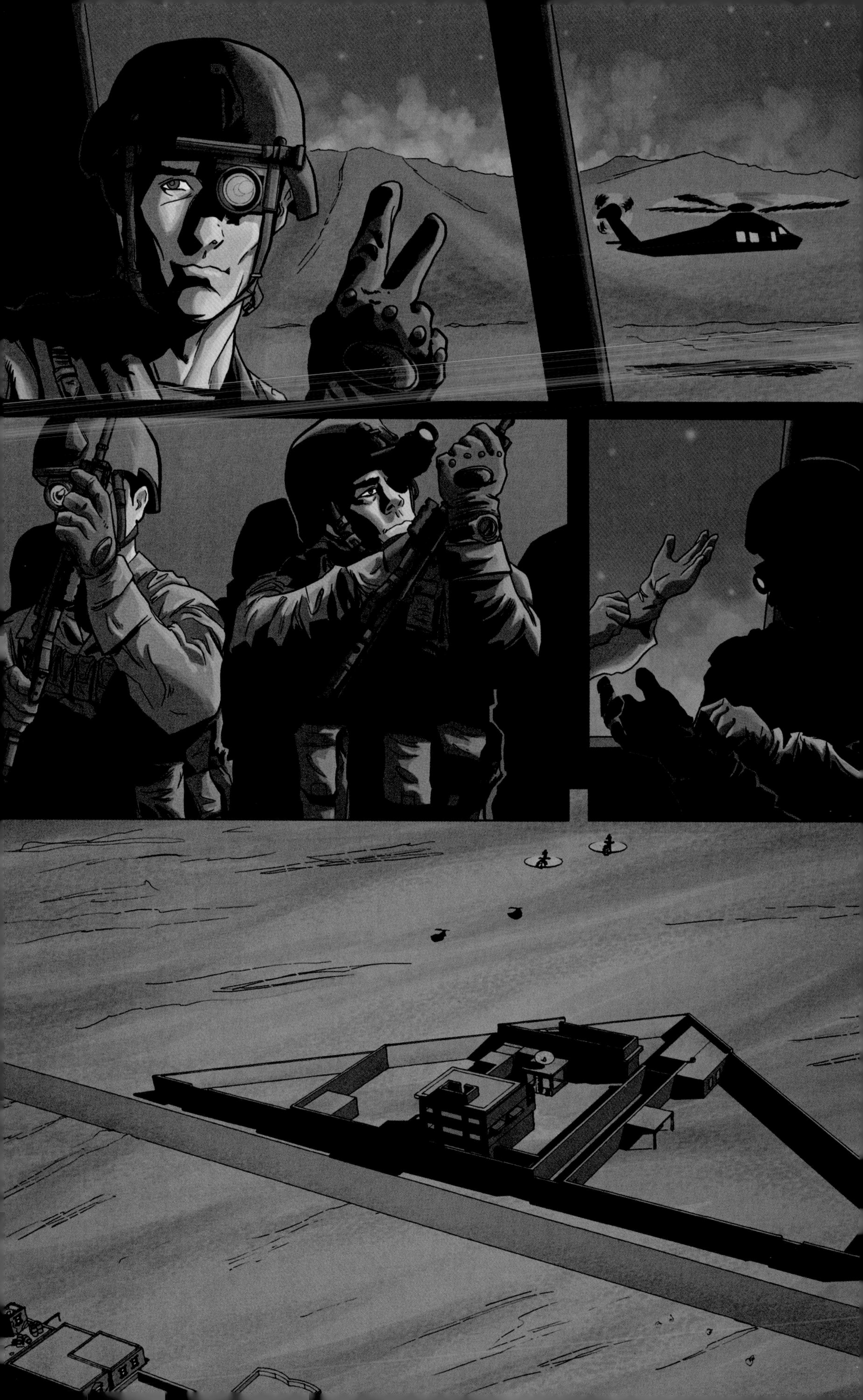

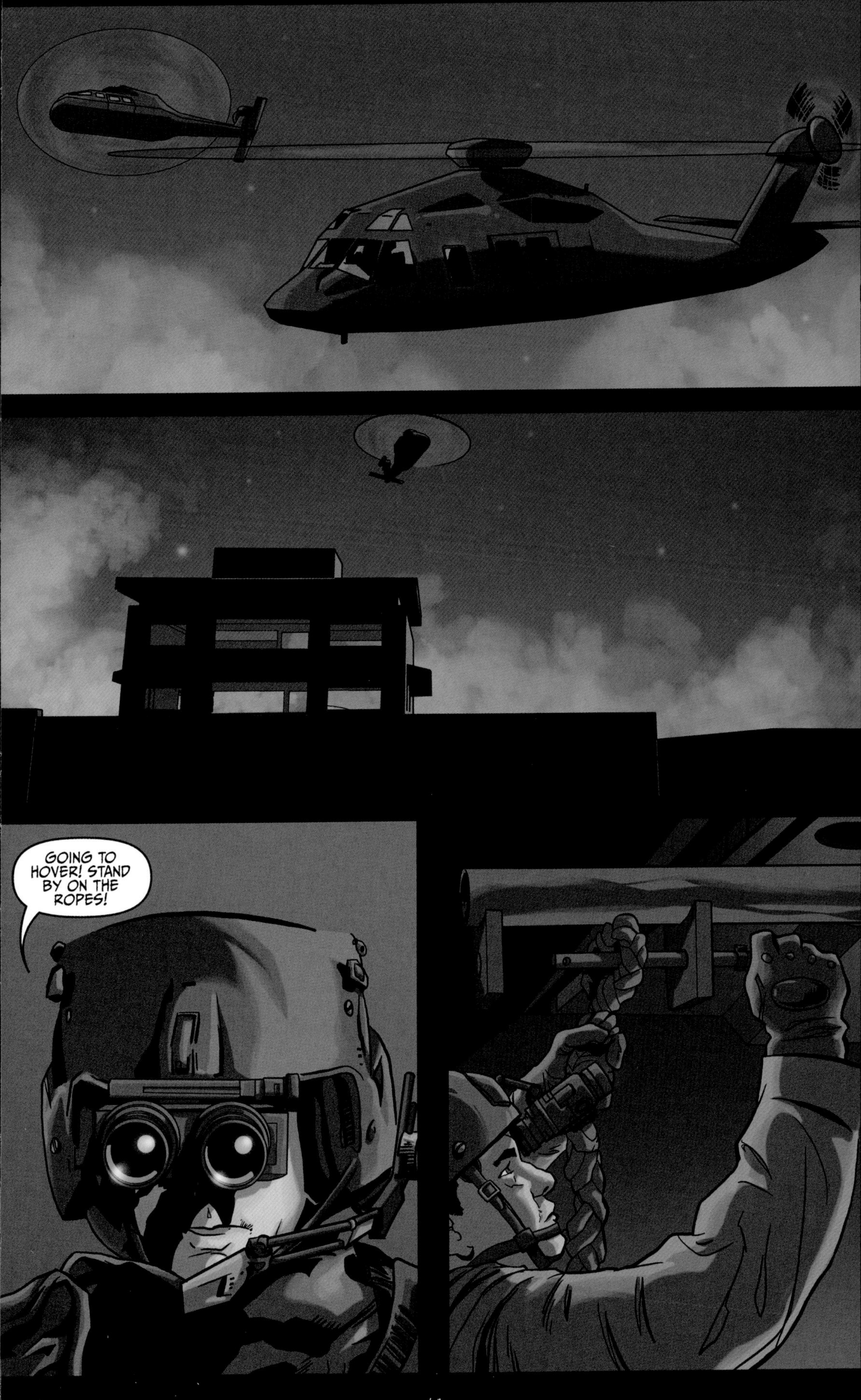
GOING TO HOVER! STAND BY ON THE ROPES!

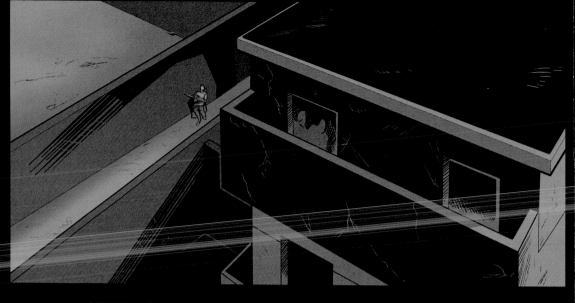

HM?!

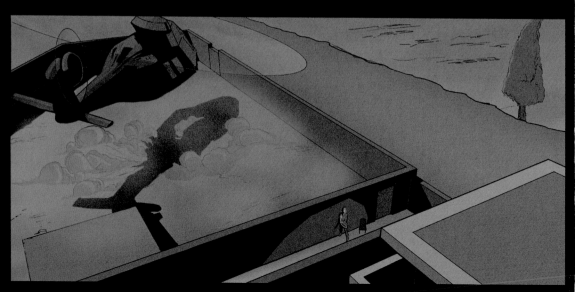

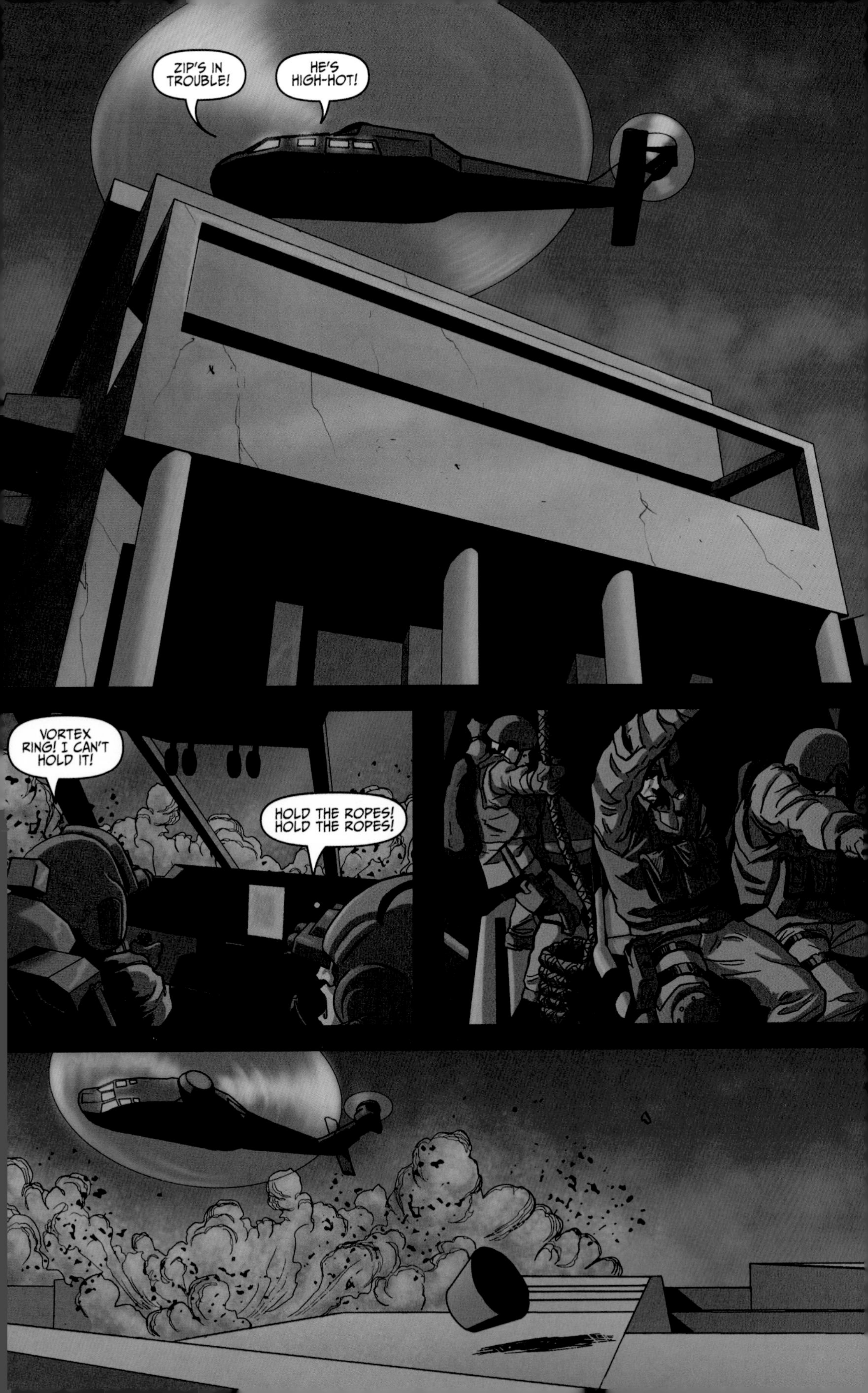
ZIP'S IN TROUBLE!
HE'S HIGH-HOT!
VORTEX RING! I CAN'T HOLD IT!
HOLD THE ROPES! HOLD THE ROPES!

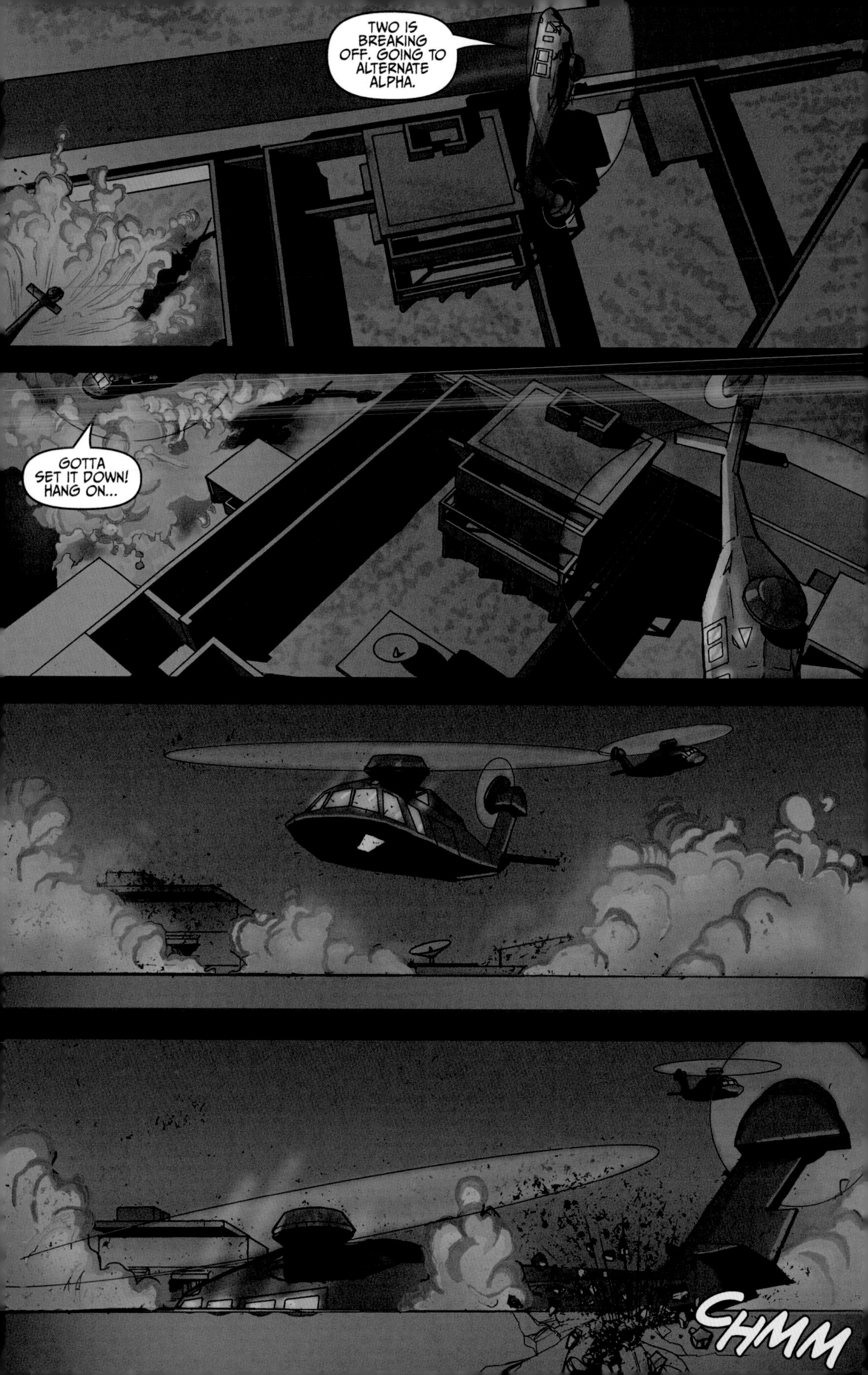
TWO IS BREAKING OFF. GOING TO ALTERNATE ALPHA.
GOTTA SET IT DOWN! HANG ON...
CHMM

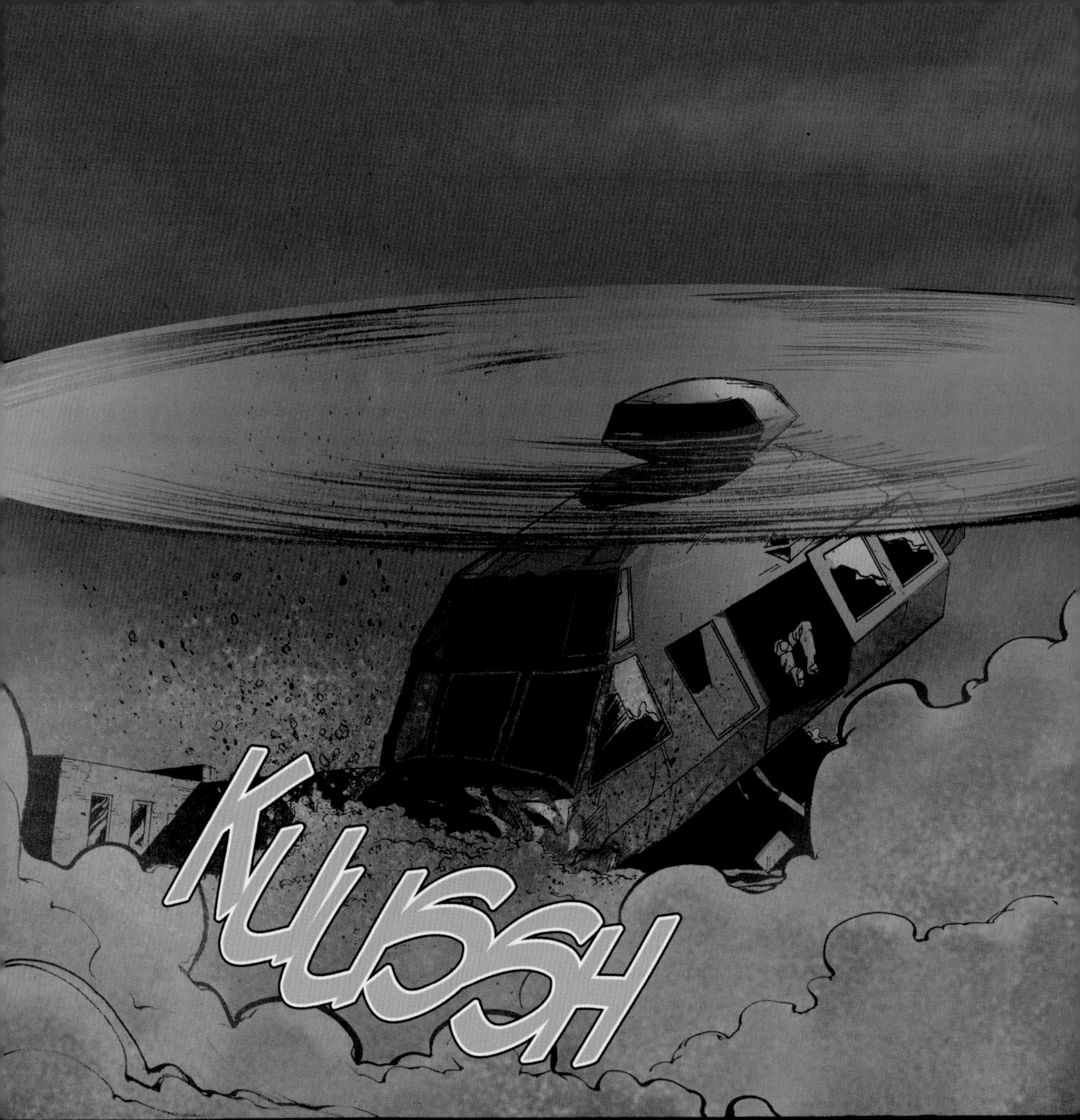
KUUSSH

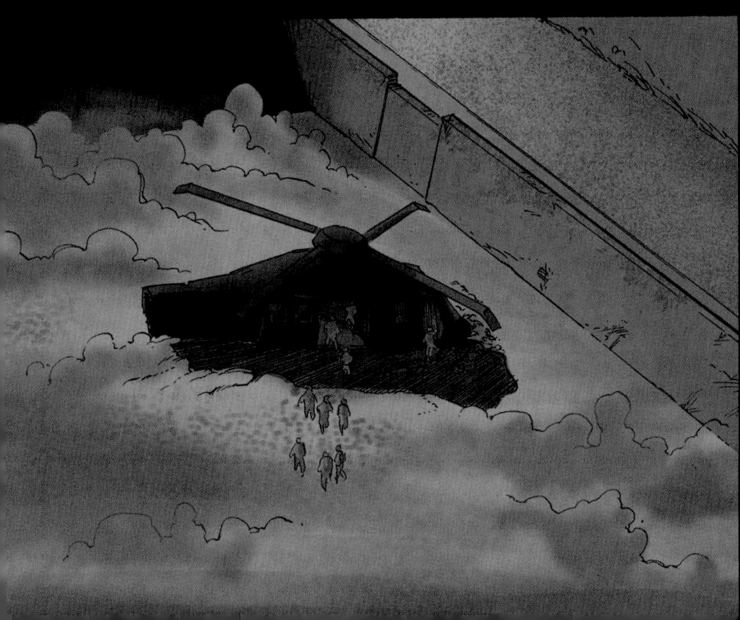

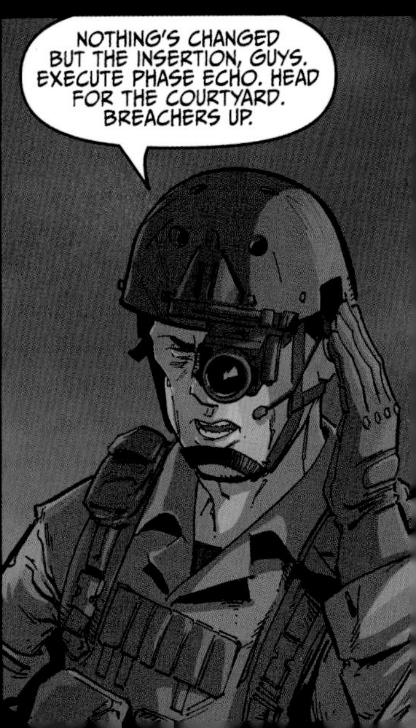
NOTHING'S CHANGED BUT THE INSERTION, GUYS. EXECUTE PHASE ECHO. HEAD FOR THE COURTYARD. BREACHERS UP.

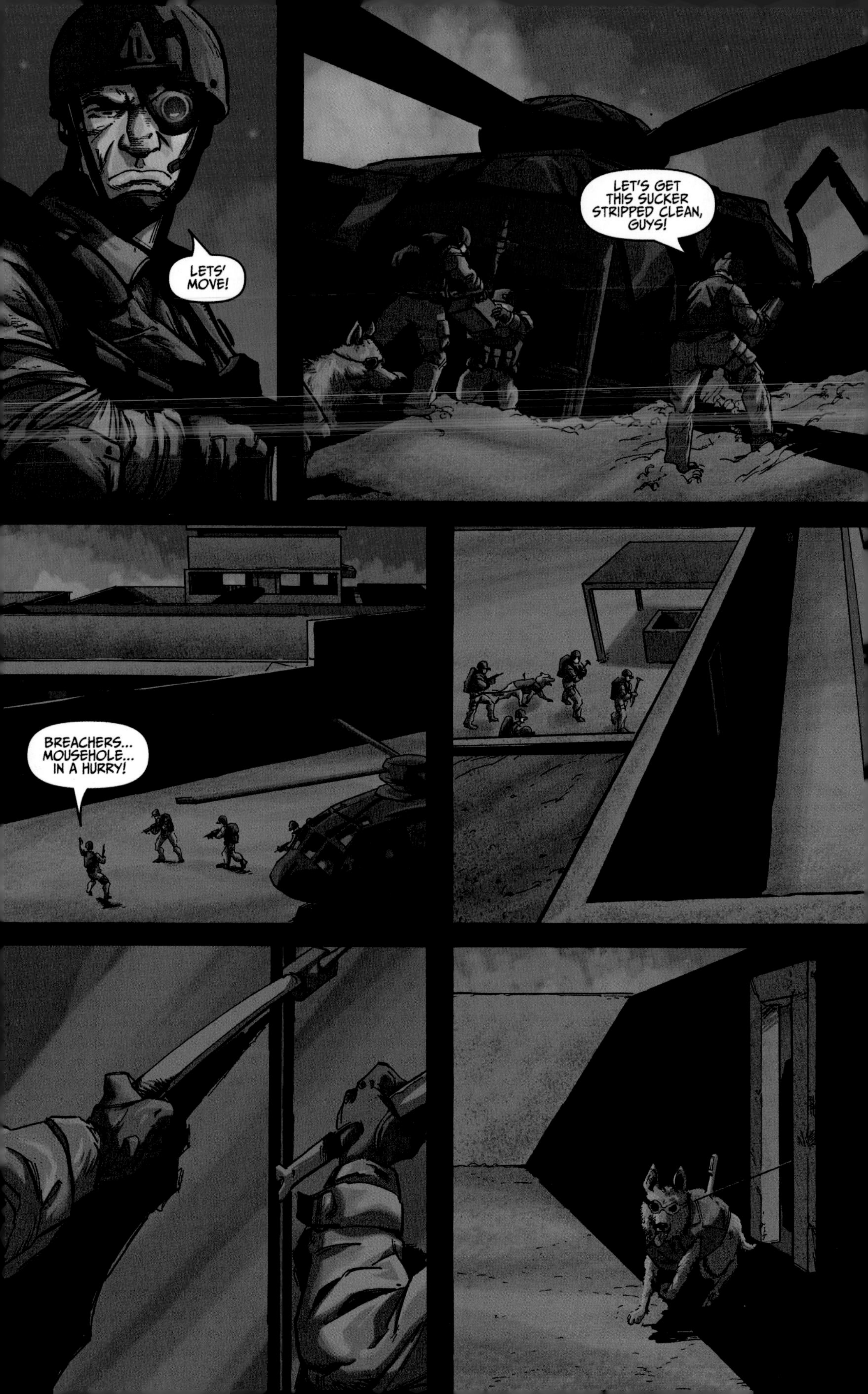
LETS' MOVE!
LET'S GET THIS SUCKER STRIPPED CLEAN, GUYS!
BREACHERS... MOUSEHOLE... IN A HURRY!

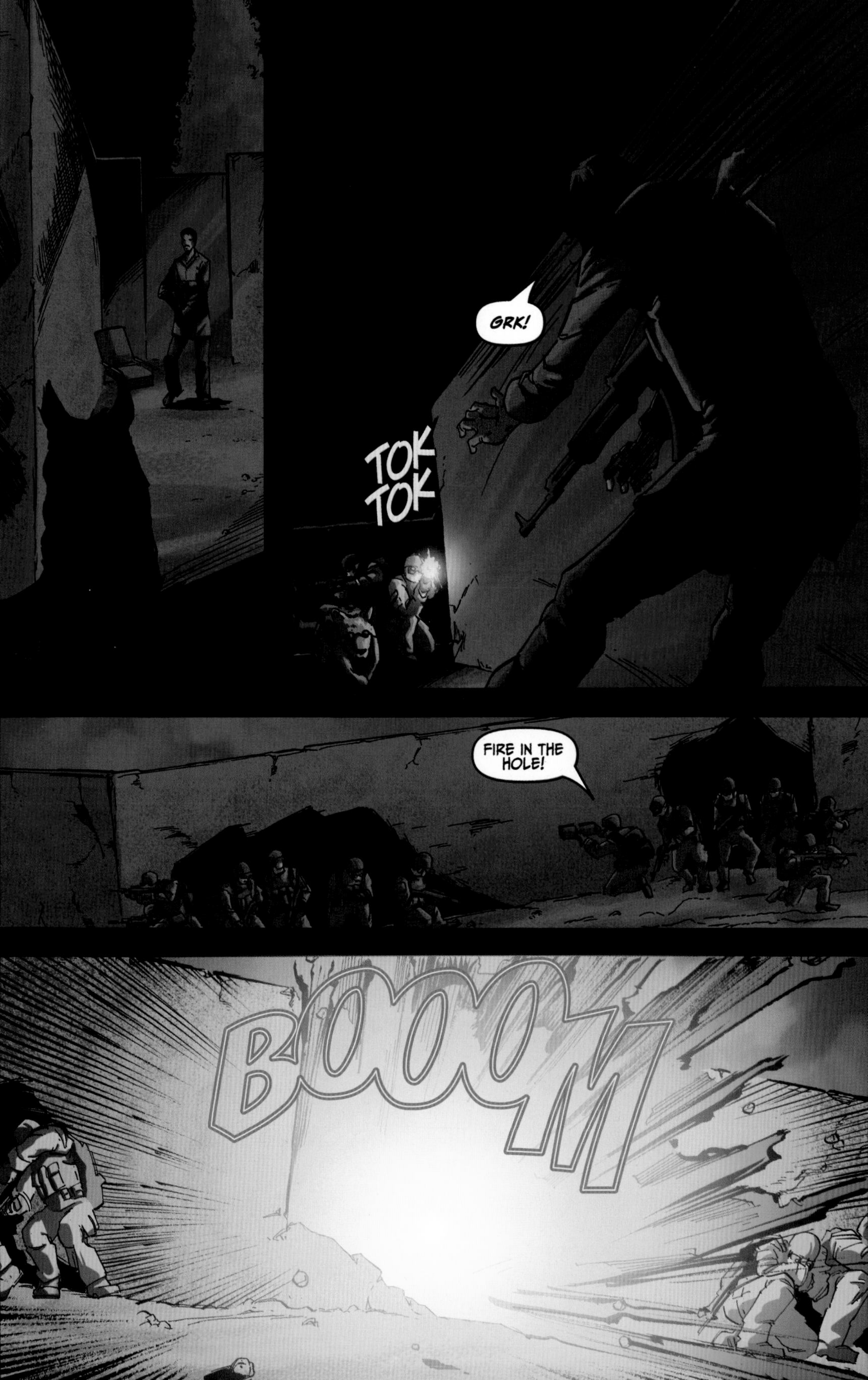
GRK!
TOK TOK
FIRE IN THE HOLE!
BOOOM

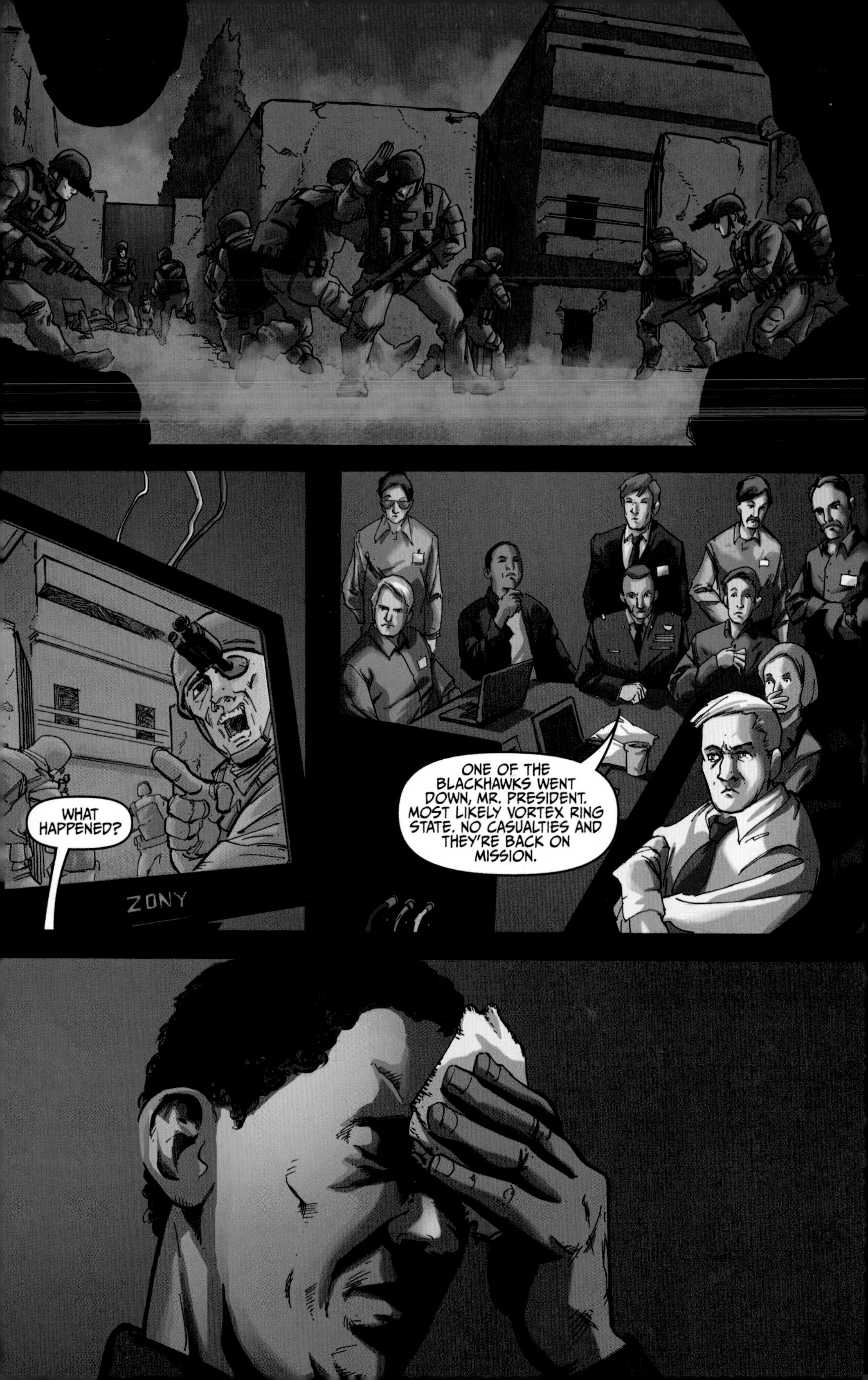
WHAT HAPPENED?
ZONY
ONE OF THE BLACKHAWKS WENT DOWN, MR. PRESIDENT. MOST LIKELY VORTEX RING STATE. NO CASUALTIES AND THEY'RE BACK ON MISSION.

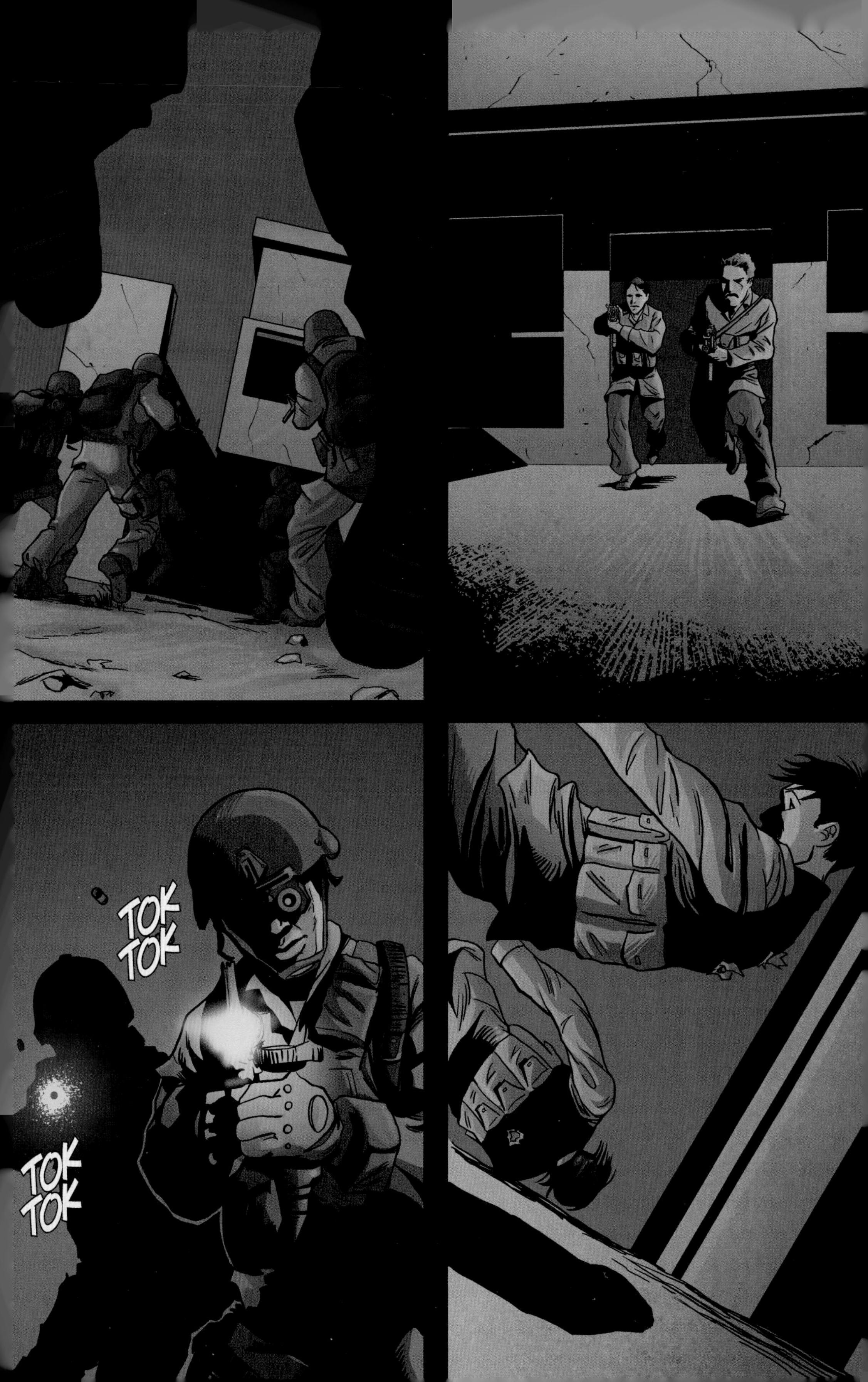
TOK
TOK
TOK
TOK

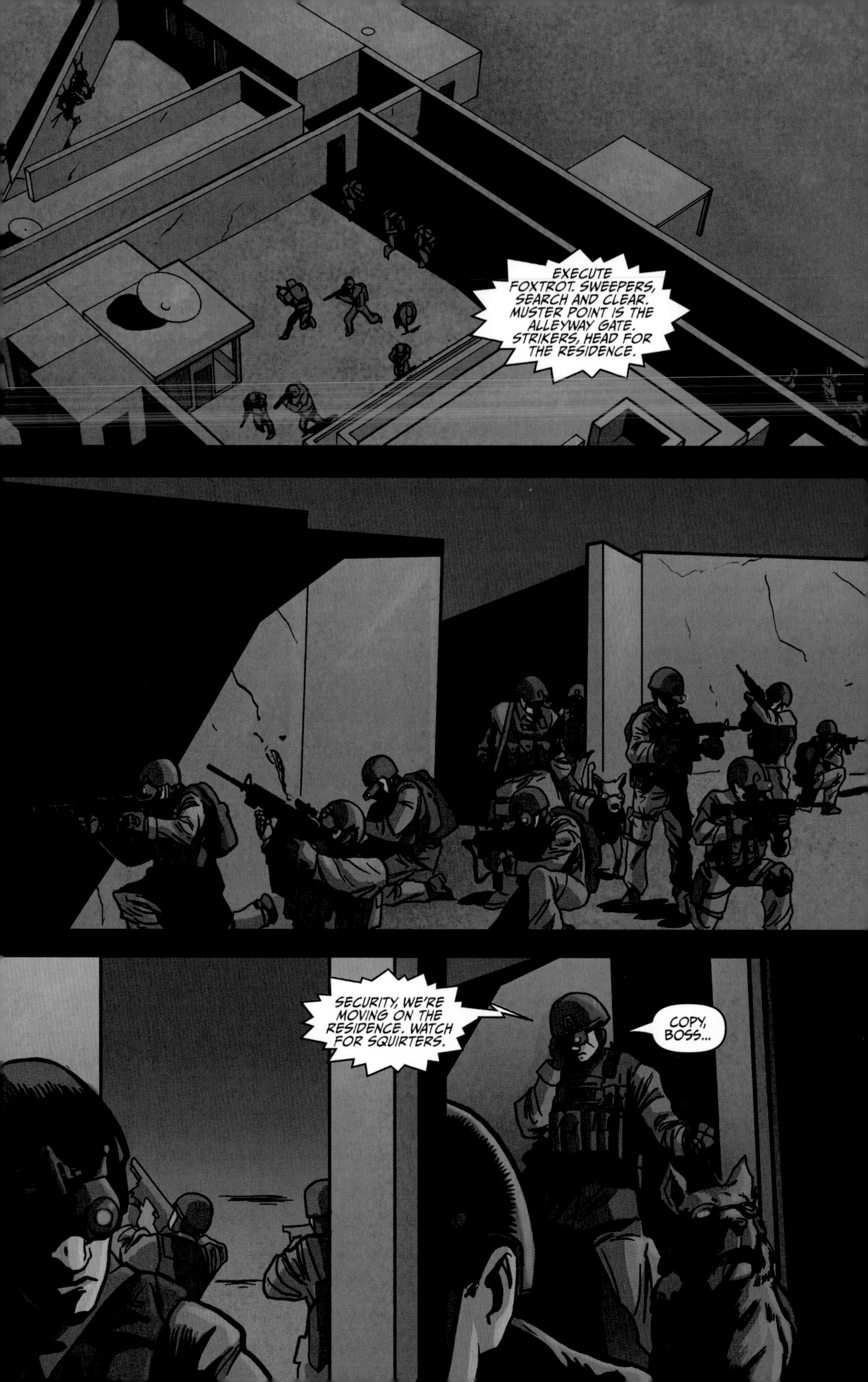
EXECUTE FOXTROT. SWEEPERS, SEARCH AND CLEAR. MUSTER POINT IS THE ALLEYWAY GATE. STRIKERS, HEAD FOR THE RESIDENCE.
SECURITY, WE'RE MOVING ON THE RESIDENCE. WATCH FOR SQUIRTERS.
COPY, BOSS...

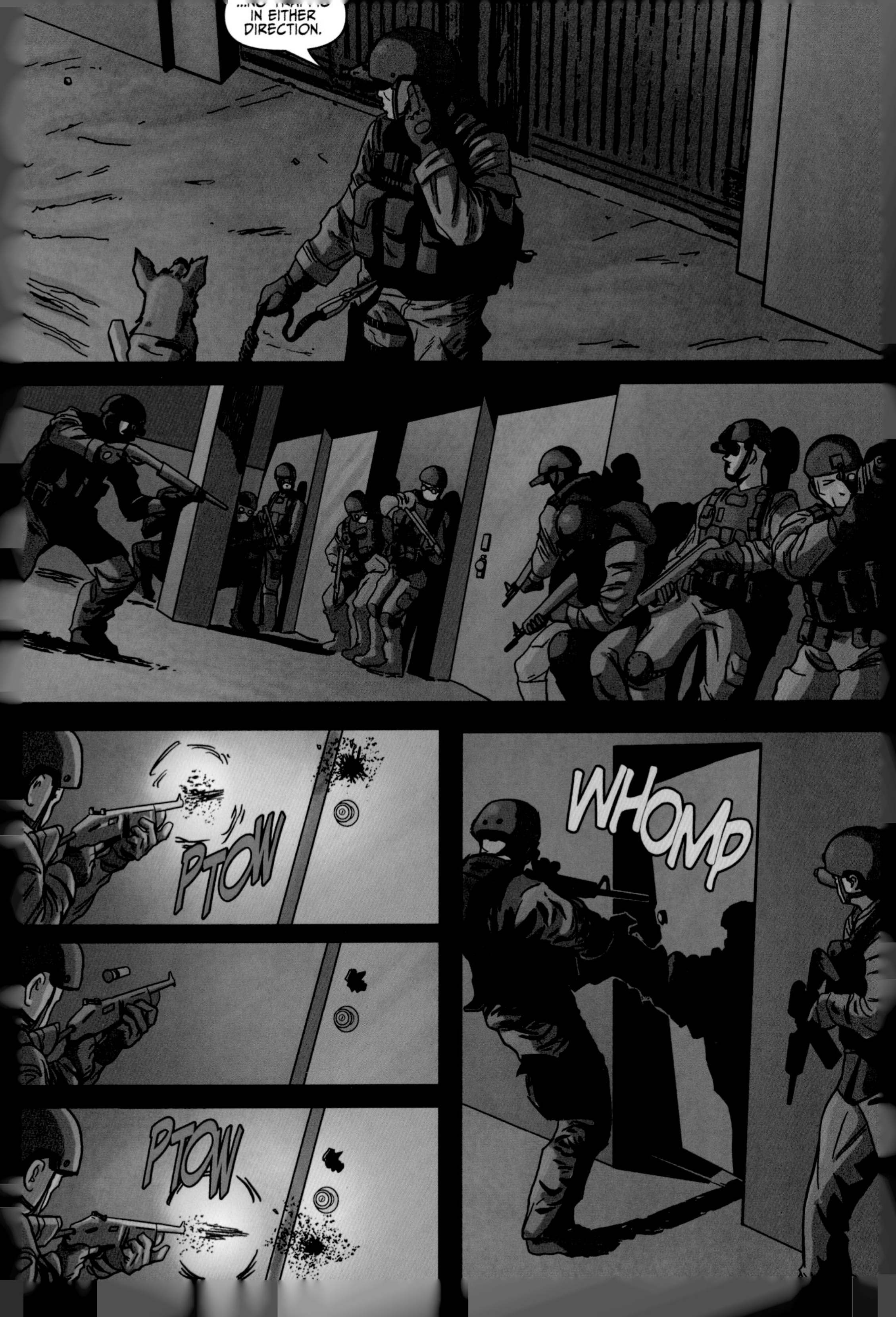
IN EITHER DIRECTION.
PTOW
PTOW
WHOMP

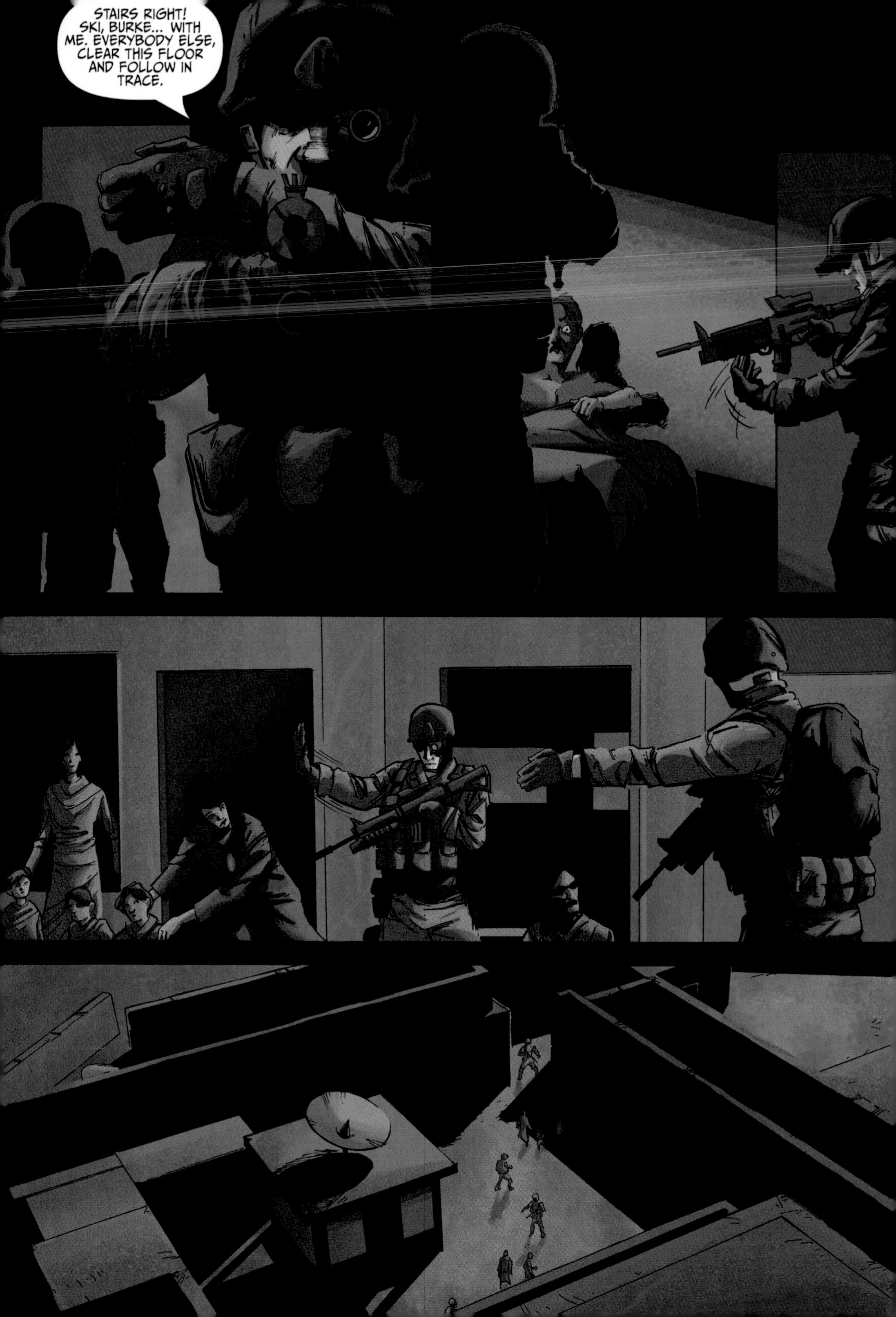
STAIRS RIGHT! SKI, BURKE... WITH ME. EVERYBODY ELSE, CLEAR THIS FLOOR AND FOLLOW IN TRACE.

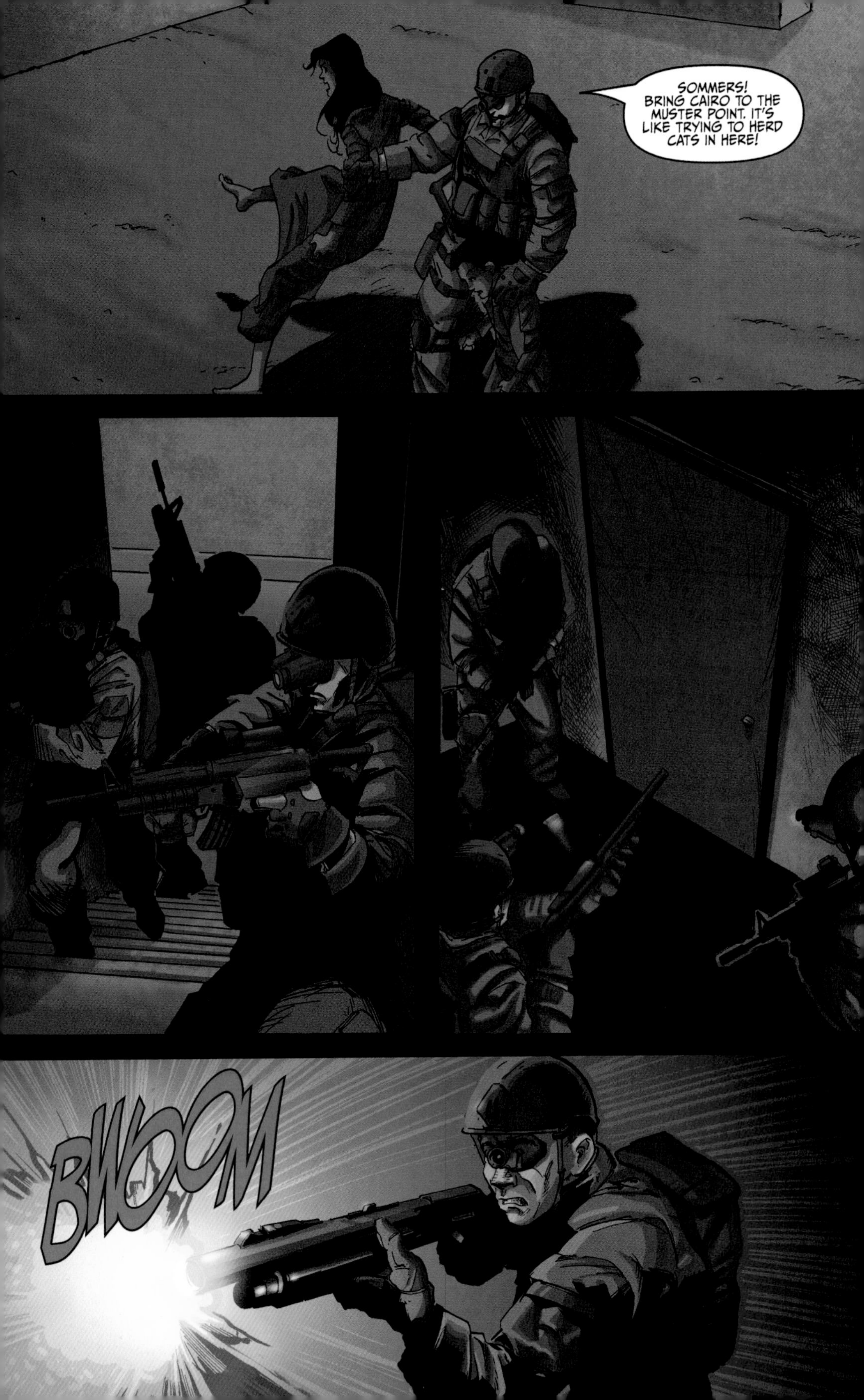
SOMMERS! BRING CAIRO TO THE MUSTER POINT. IT'S LIKE TRYING TO HERD CATS IN HERE!
BWOOM

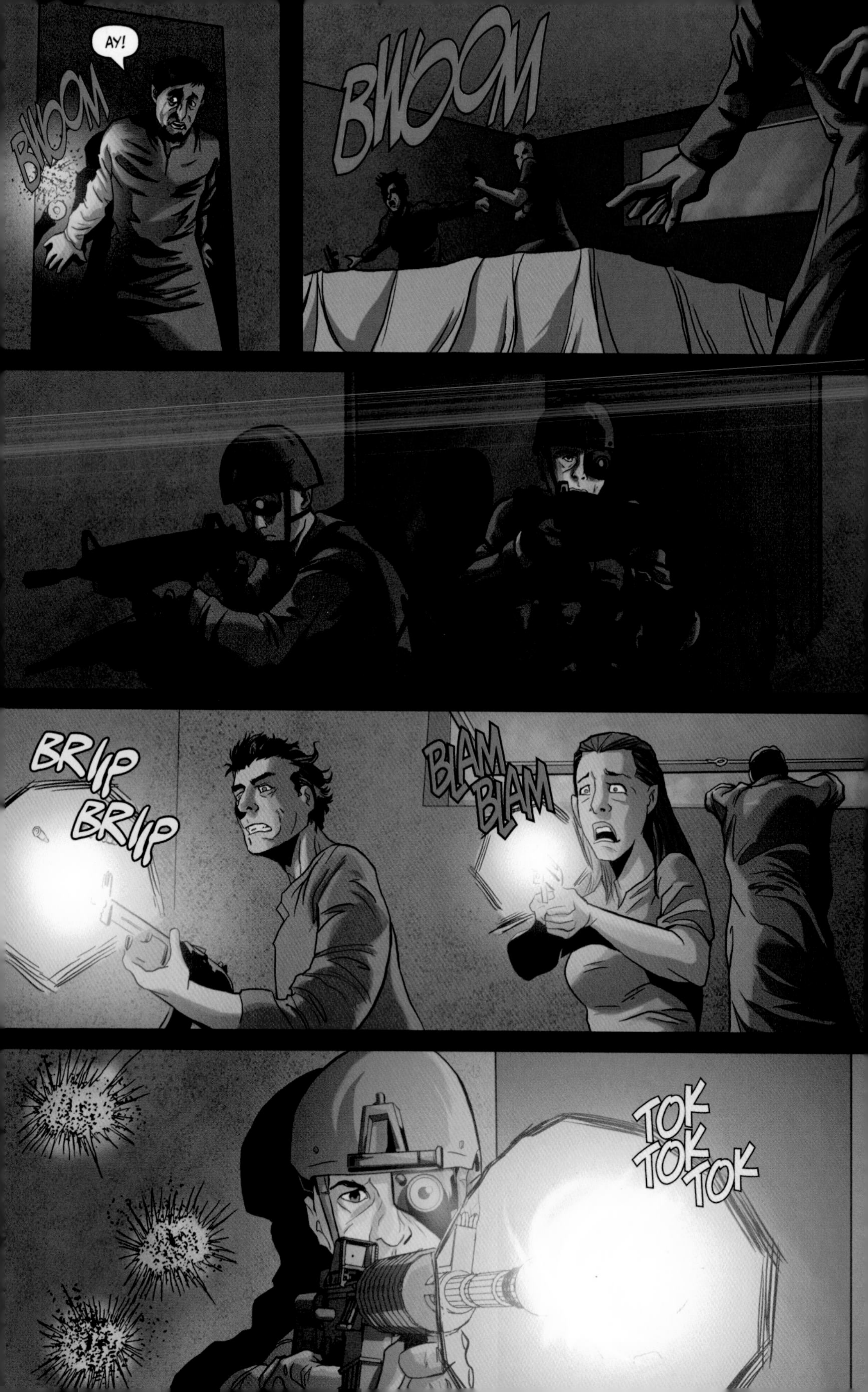
AY!
BWOOM
BWOOM
BRIIP
BRIIP
BLAM
BLAM
TOK
TOK
TOK

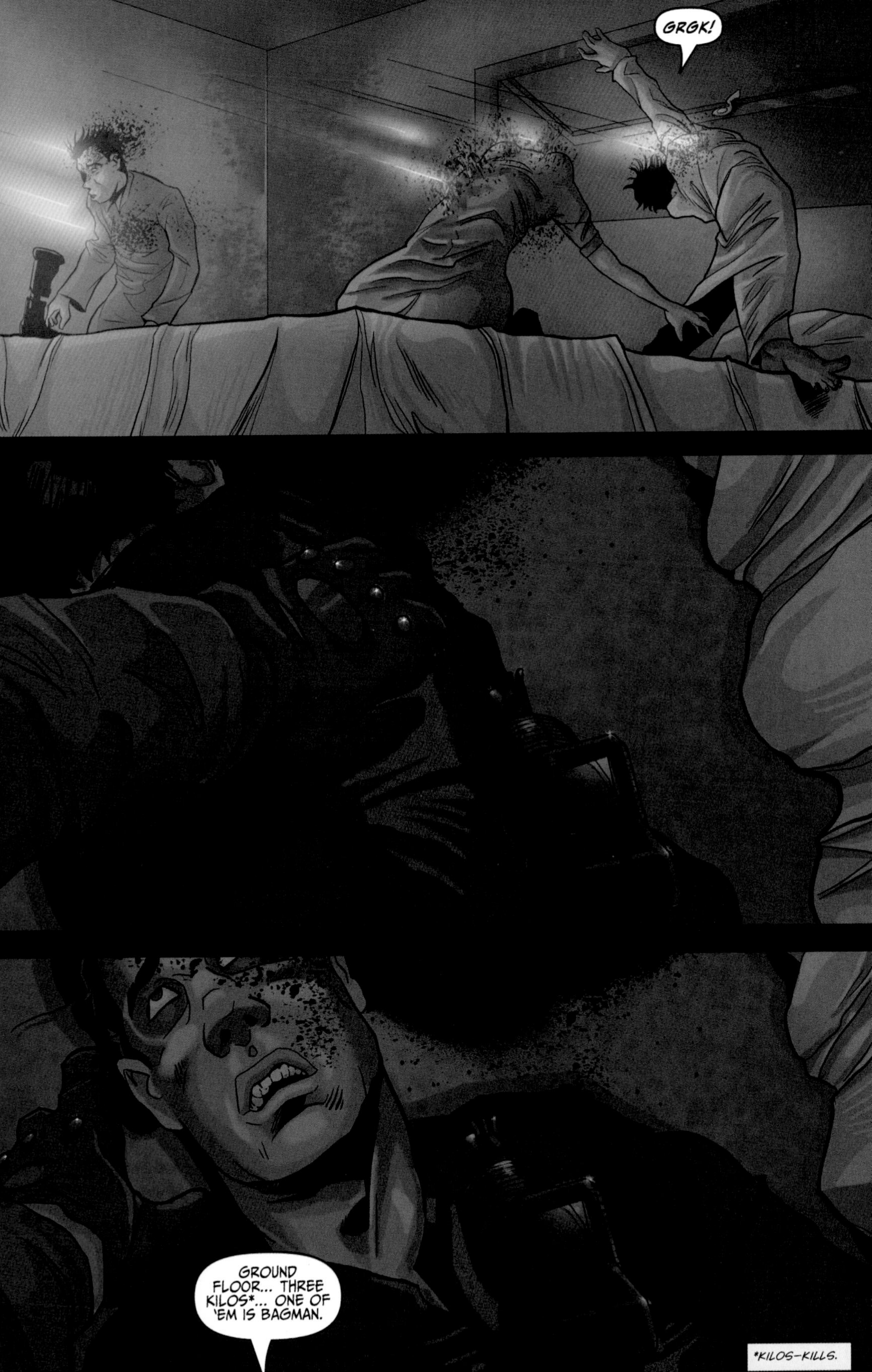
GRGK!
GROUND FLOOR... THREE KILOS*... ONE OF 'EM IS BAGMAN.
*KILOS–KILLS.

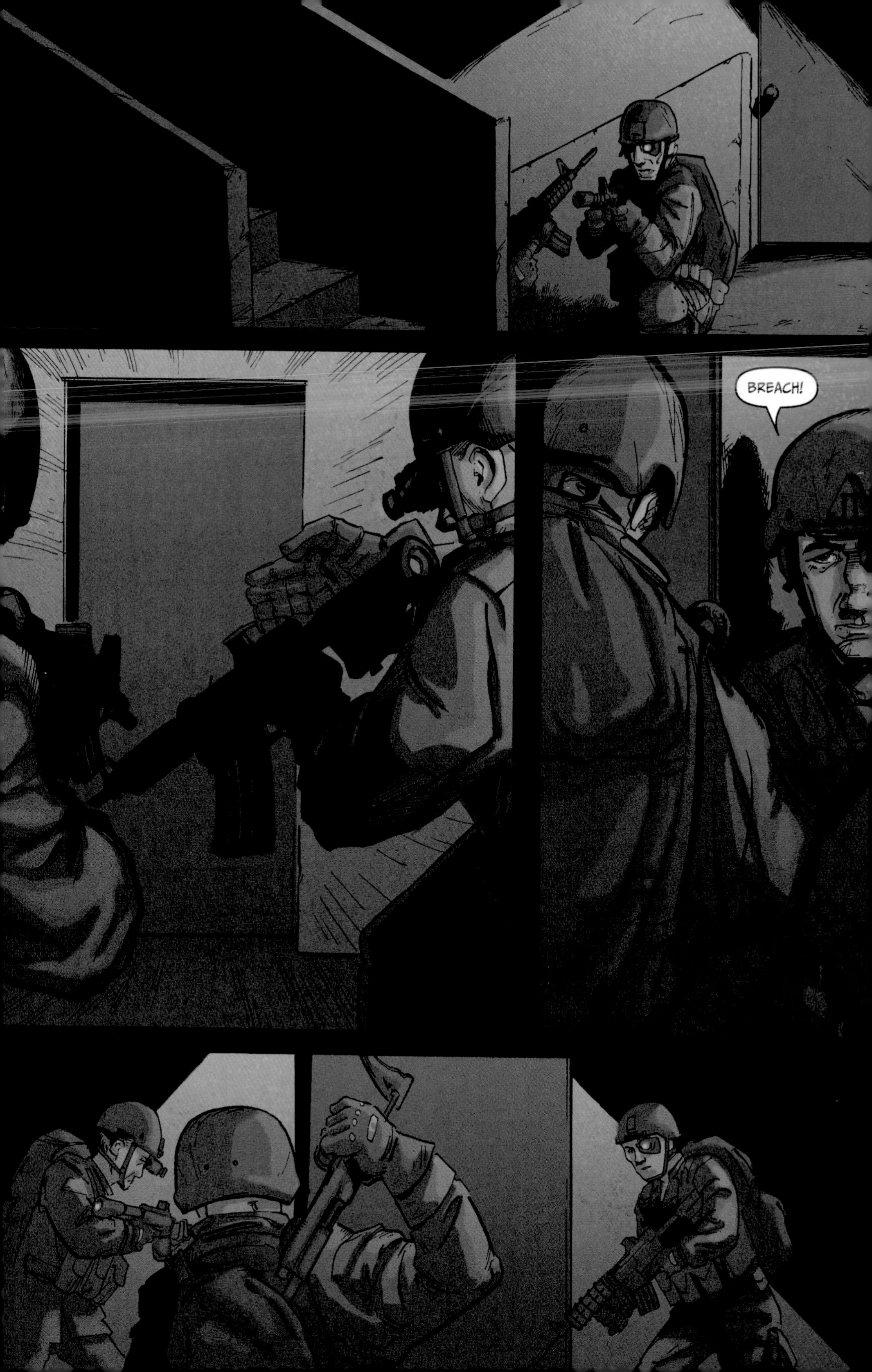
BREACH!

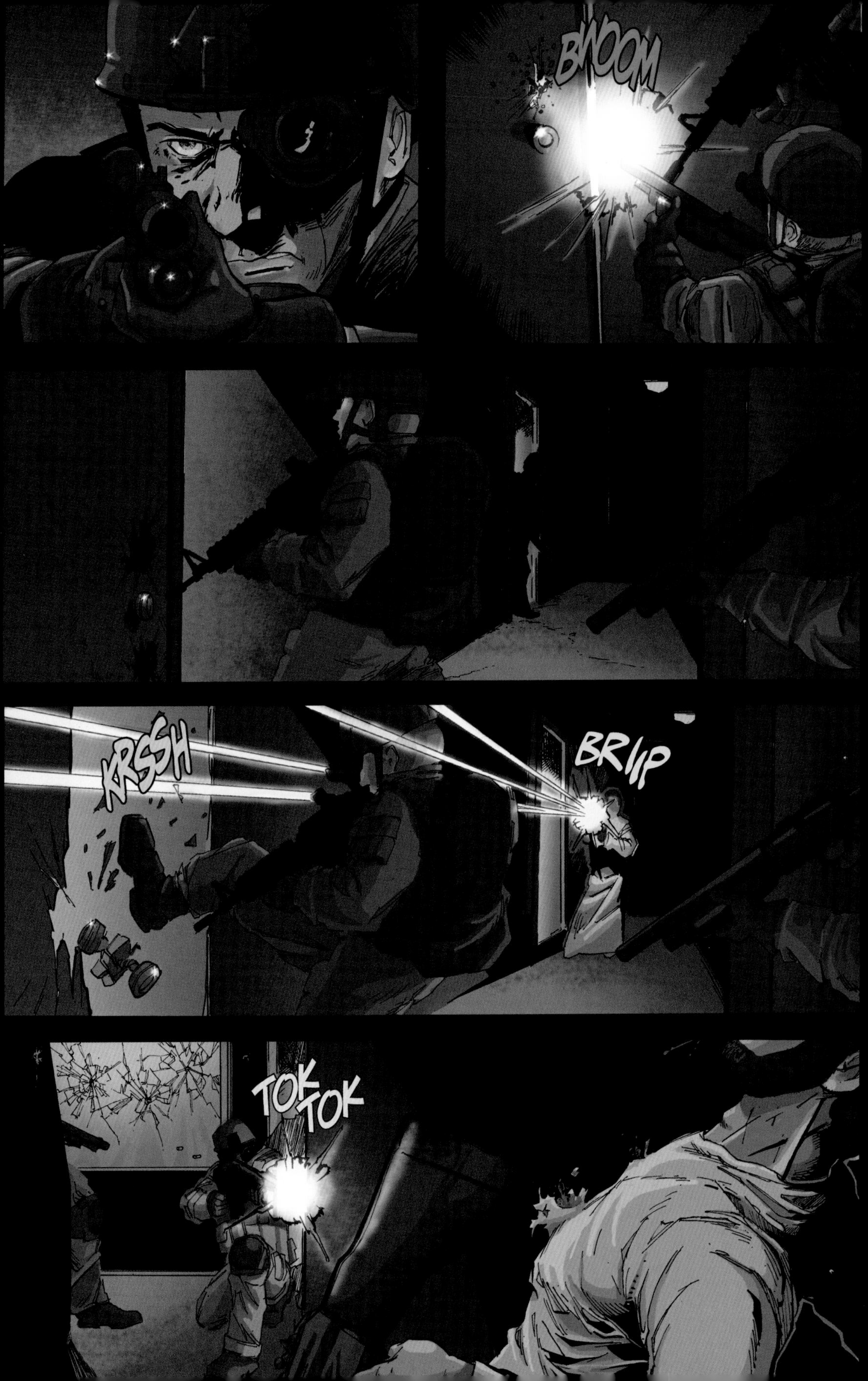
BWOOM
KRSSH
BRIIP
TOK
TOK

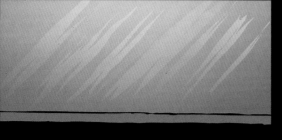

CLEAR ON THE
GROUND. WE'RE
COMIN' UP.

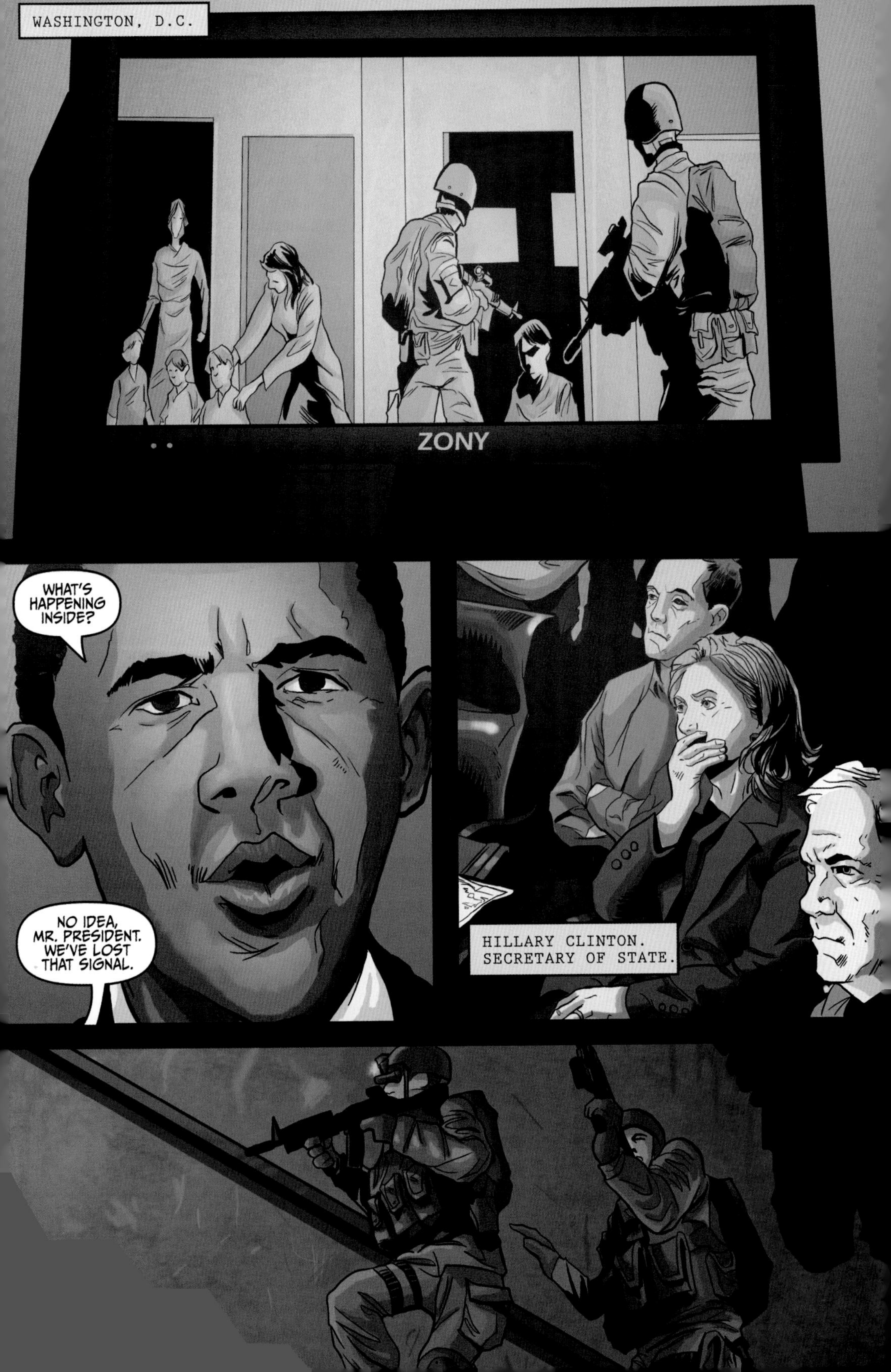
WASHINGTON, D.C.
ZONY
WHAT'S HAPPENING INSIDE?
NO IDEA, MR. PRESIDENT. WE'VE LOST THAT SIGNAL.
HILLARY CLINTON. SECRETARY OF STATE.

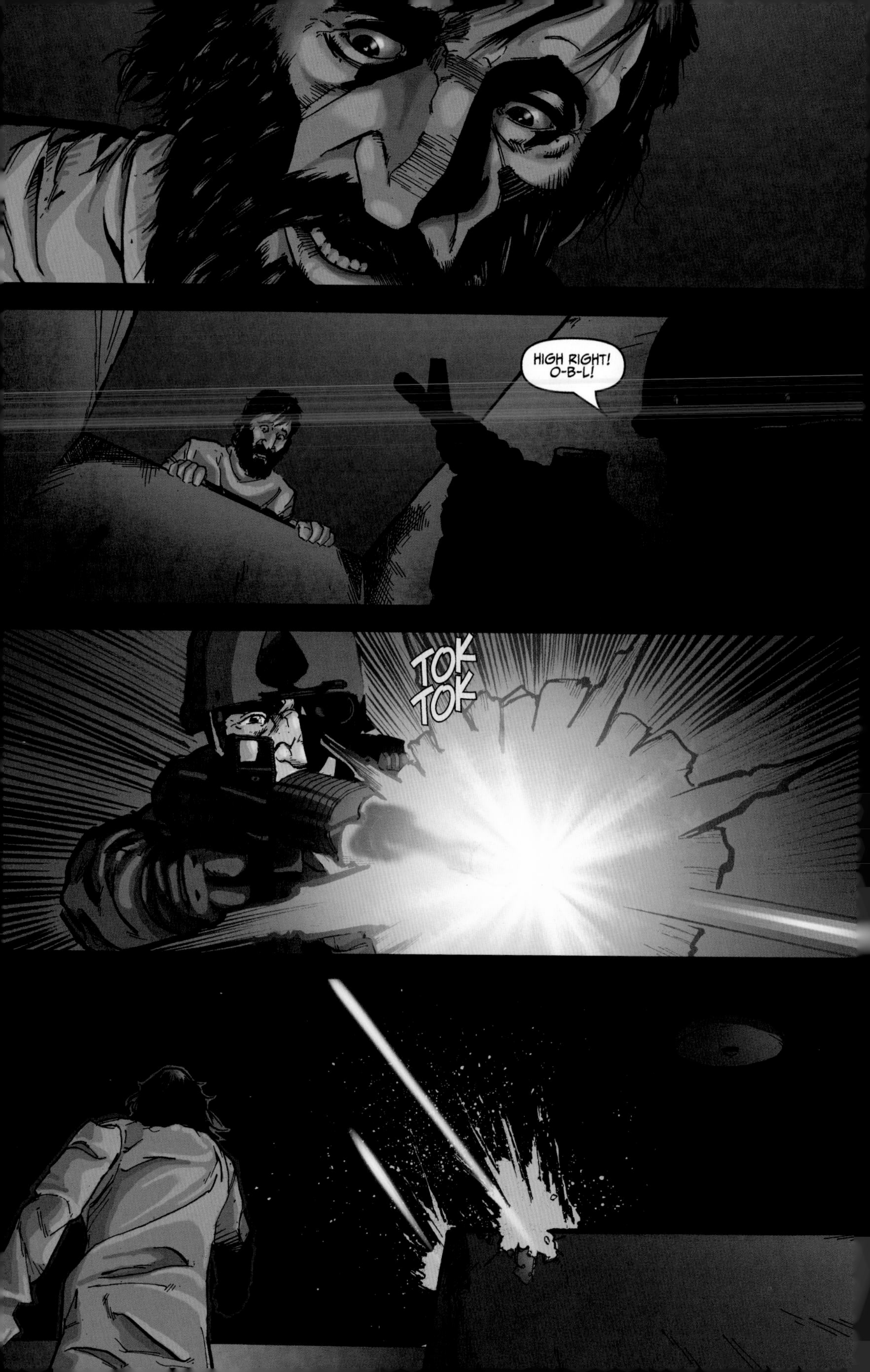
HIGH RIGHT! O-B-L!
TOK TOK

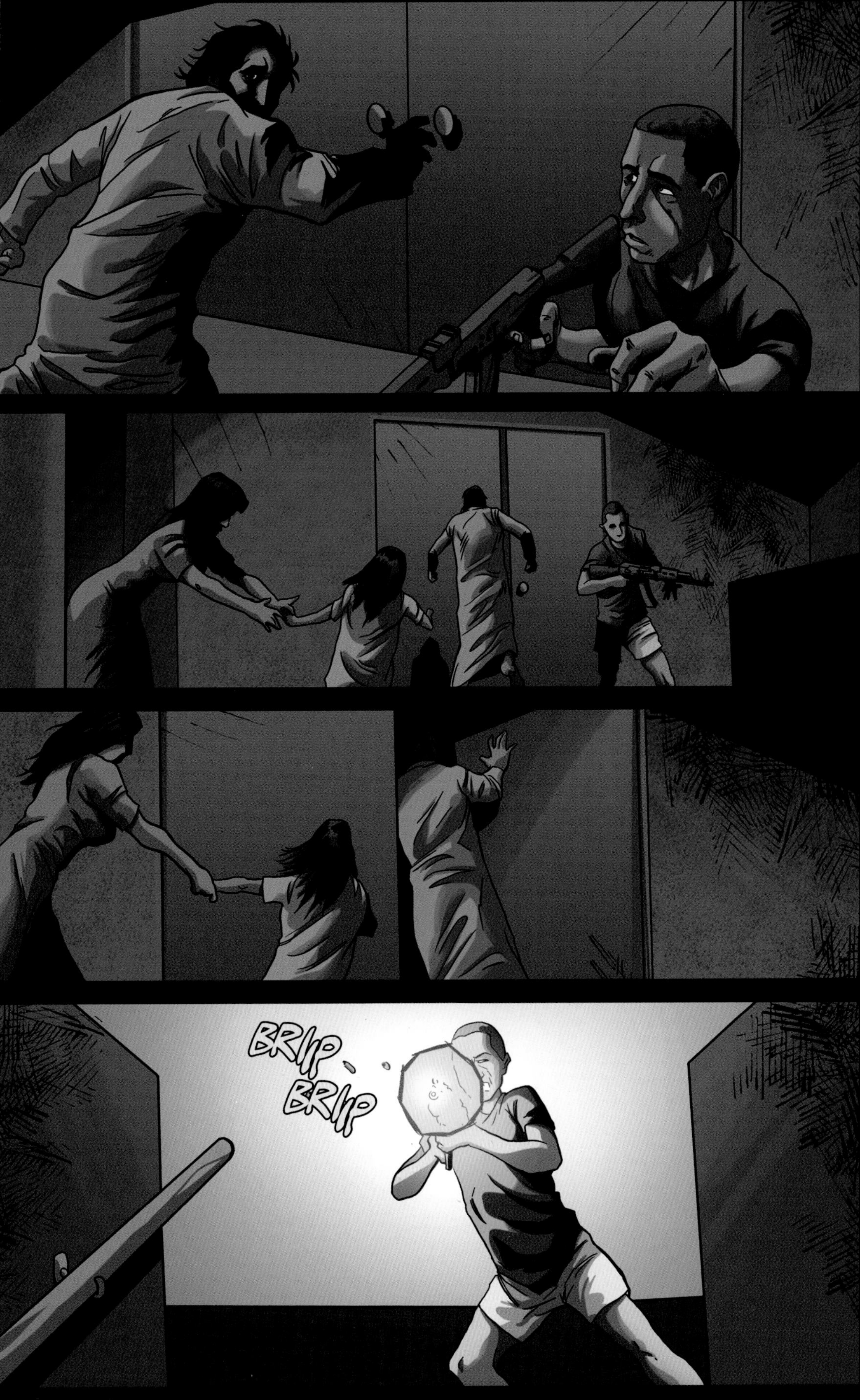
BRIIP
BRIIP

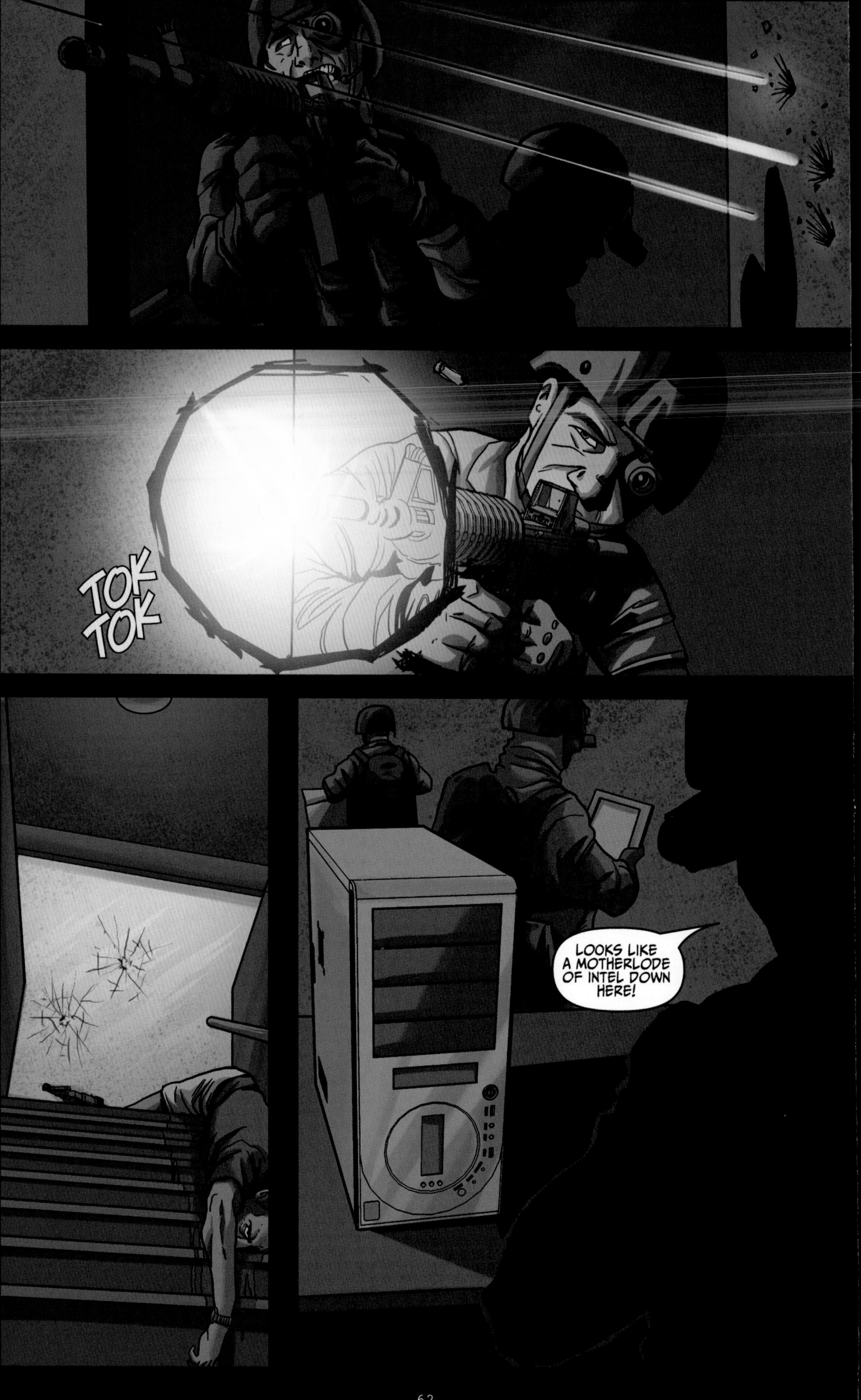
TOK
TOK
LOOKS LIKE A MOTHERLODE OF INTEL DOWN HERE!

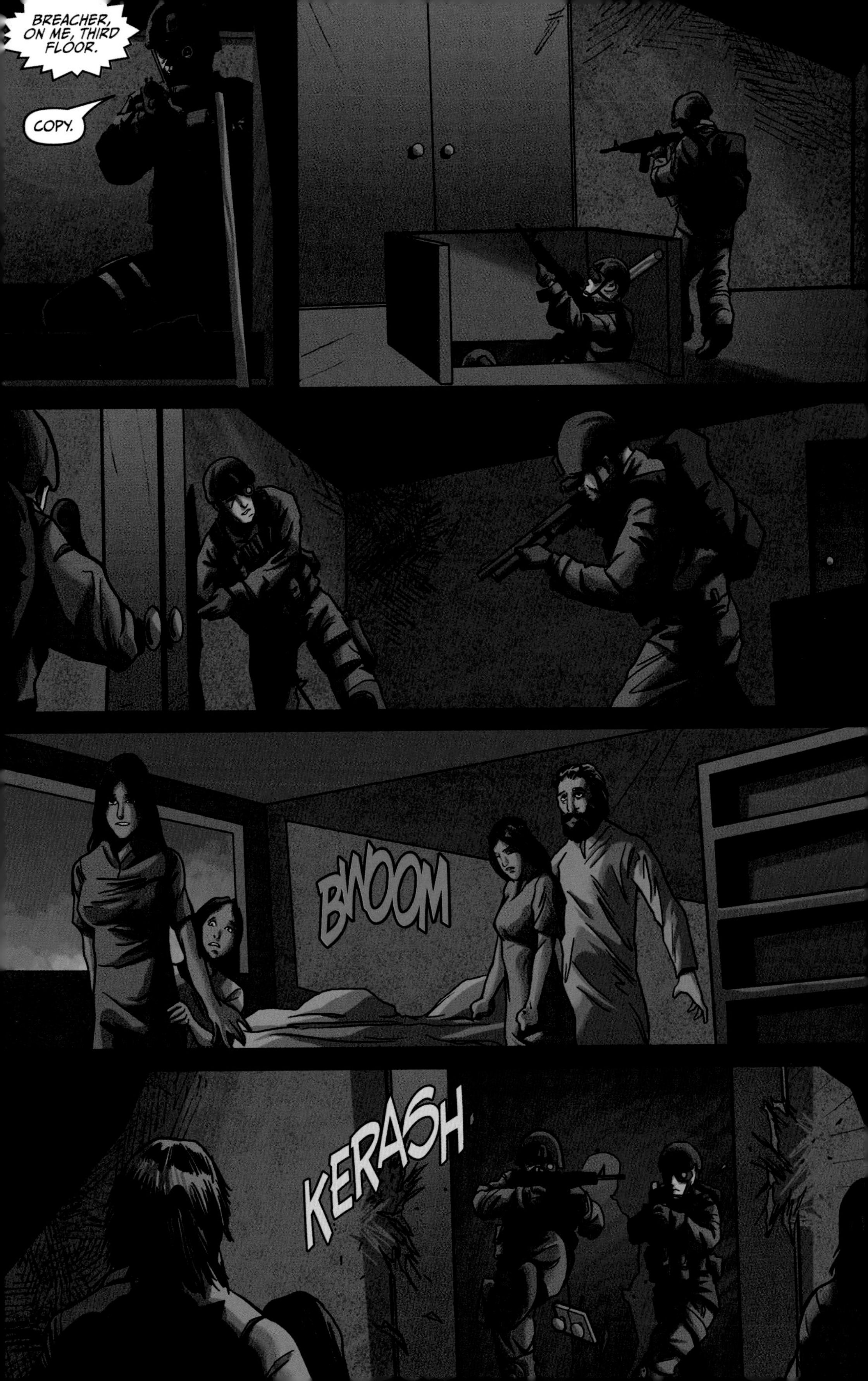
BREACHER, ON ME, THIRD FLOOR.
COPY.
BWOOM
KERASH

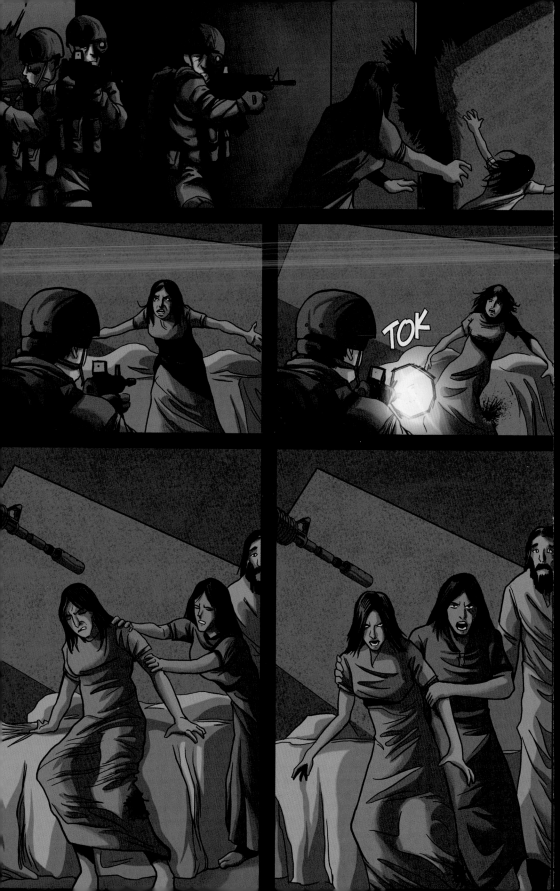

TOK

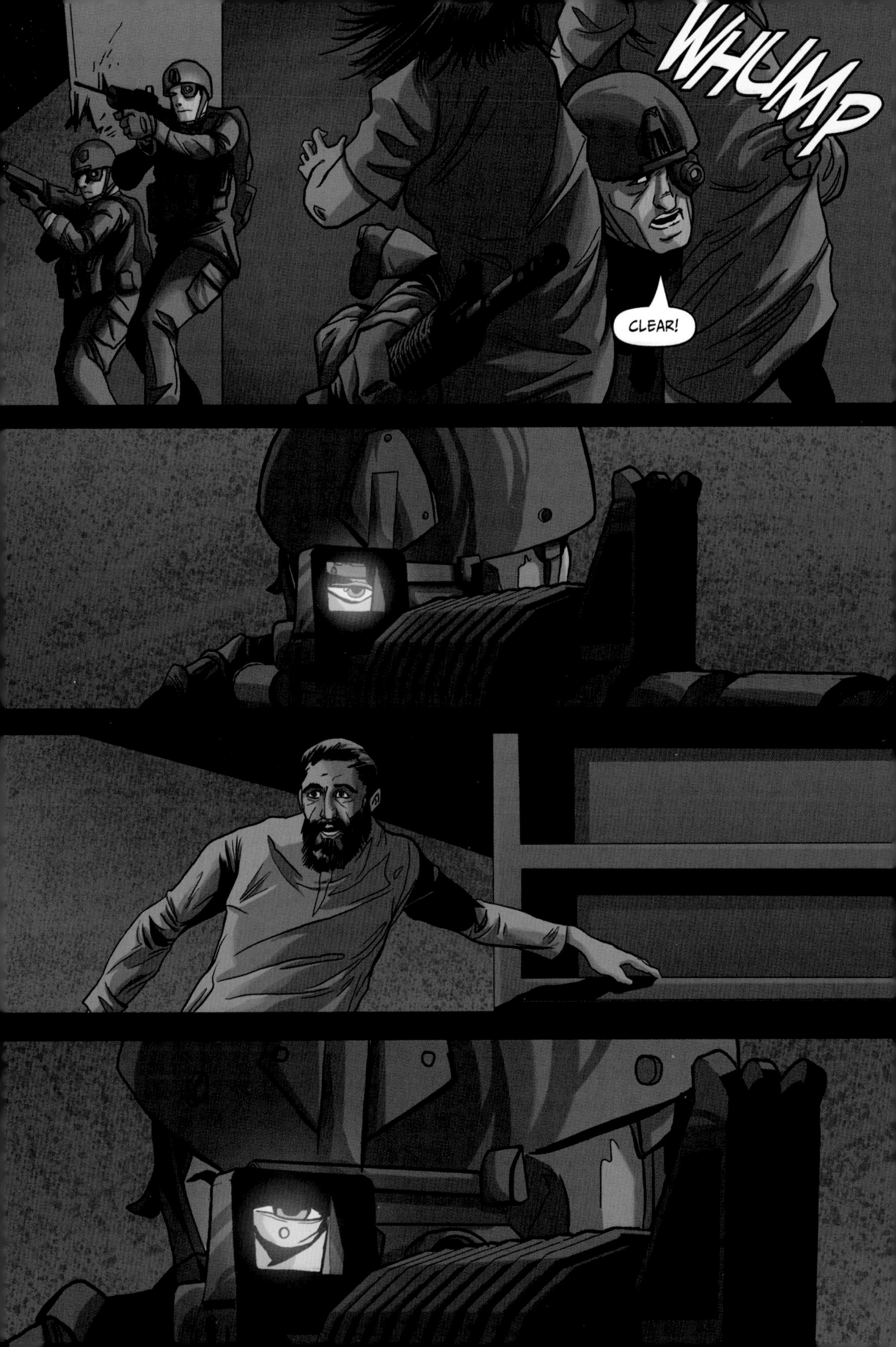
WHUMP
CLEAR!

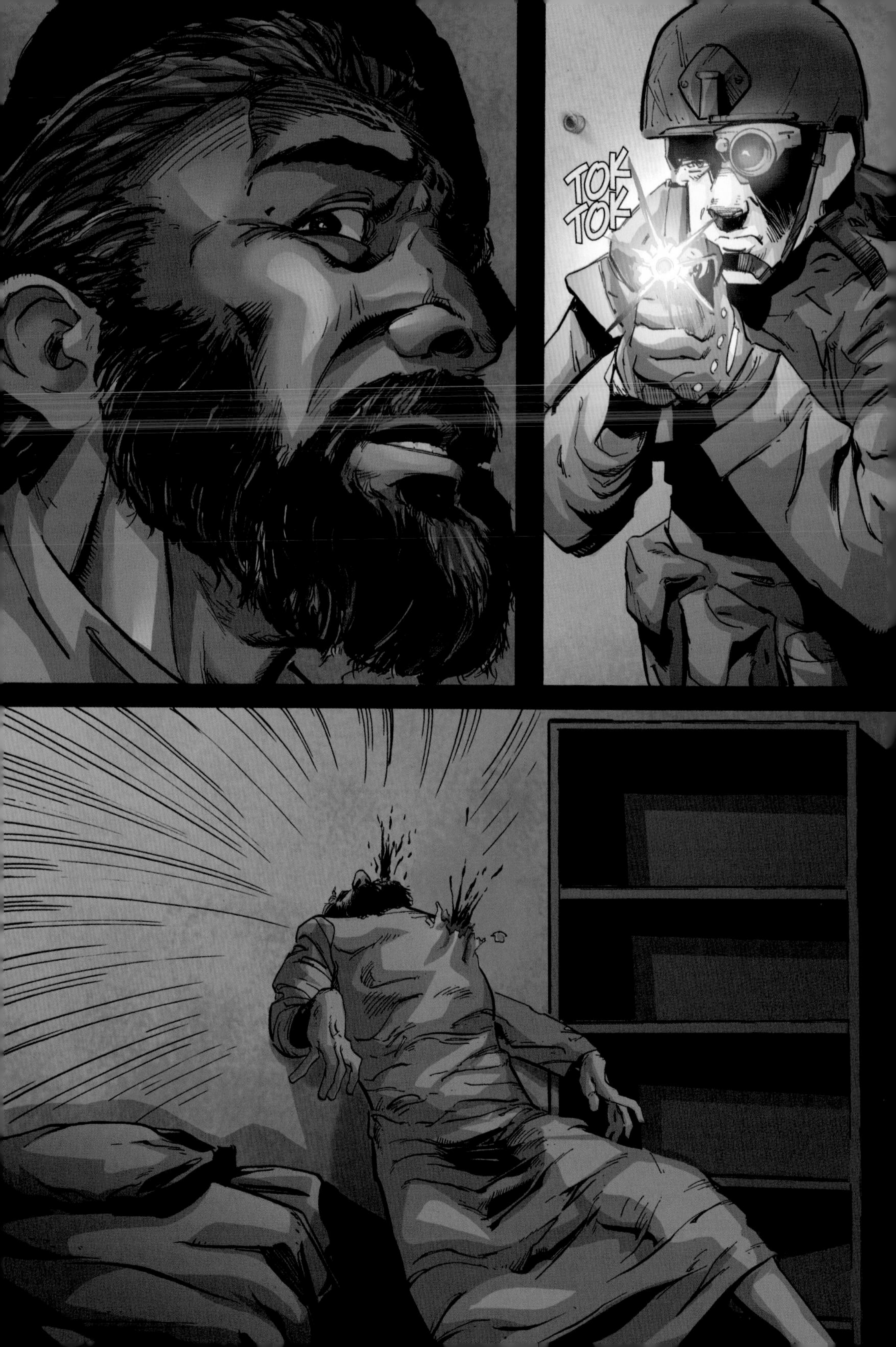
TOK TOK

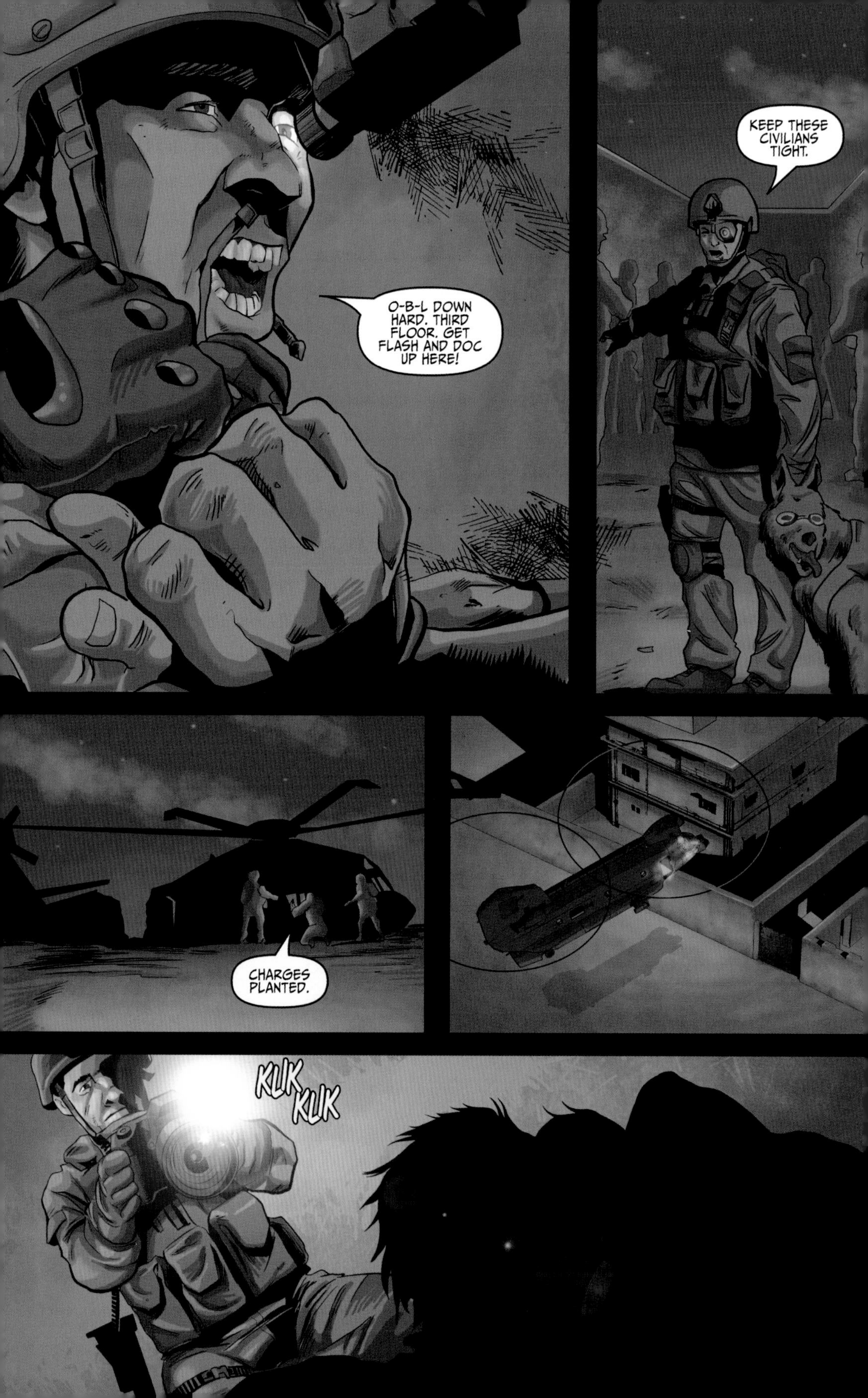
O-B-L DOWN HARD. THIRD FLOOR. GET FLASH AND DOC UP HERE!
KEEP THESE CIVILIANS TIGHT.
CHARGES PLANTED.
KLIK KLIK

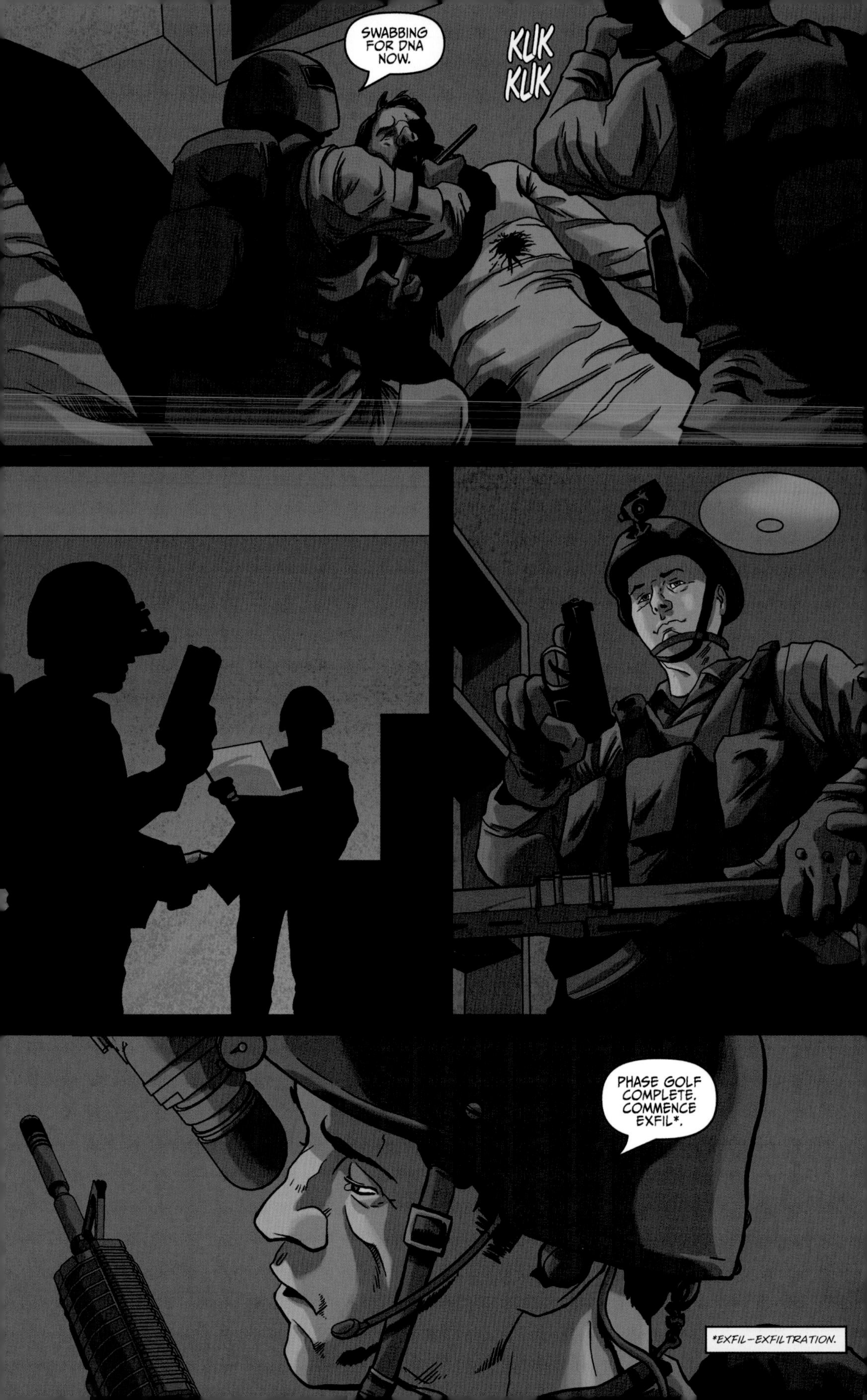
SWABBING FOR DNA NOW.
KLIK KLIK
PHASE GOLF COMPLETE. COMMENCE EXFIL*.
*EXFIL—EXFILTRATION.

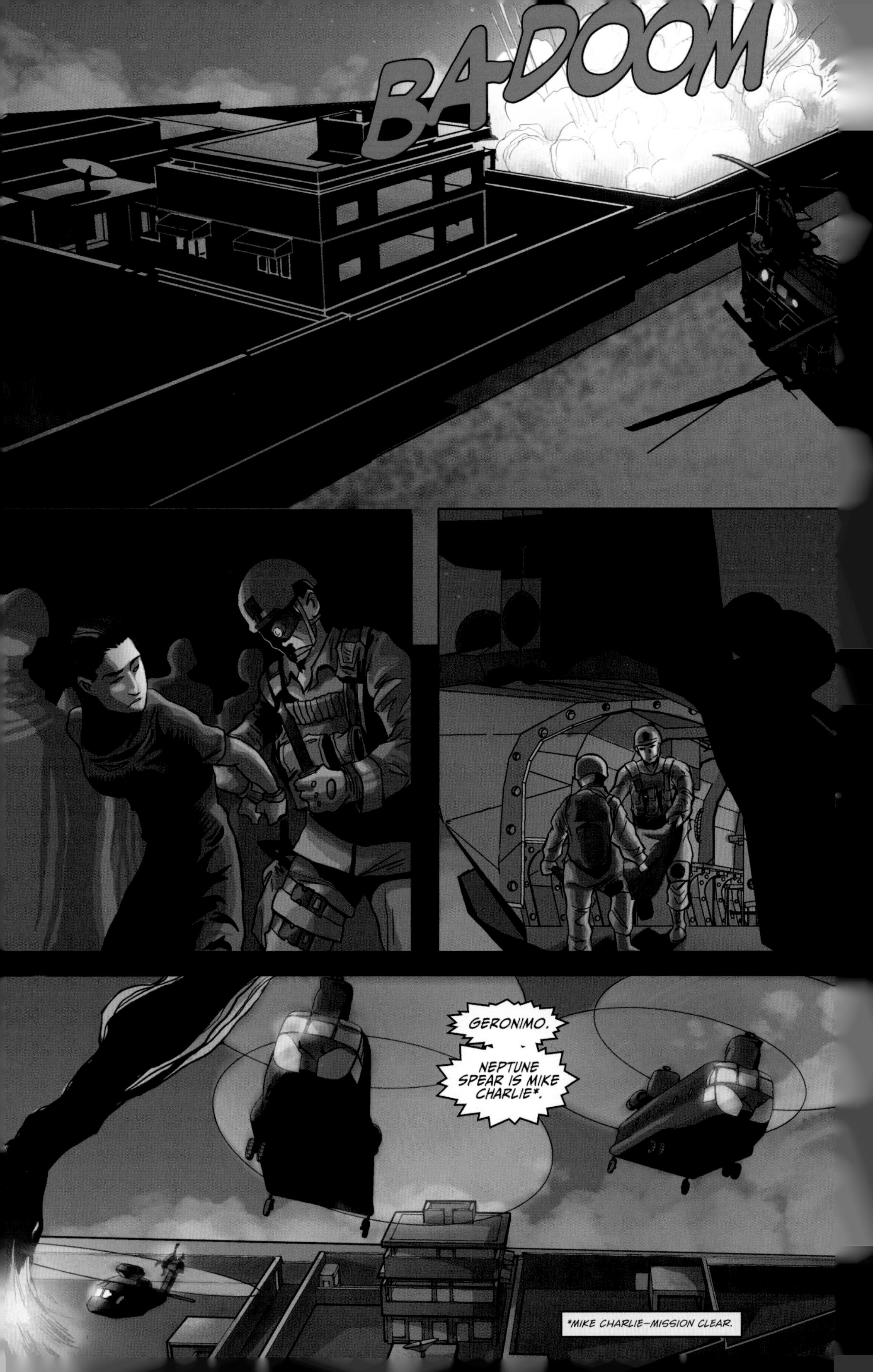
BA-DOOM
GERONIMO.
NEPTUNE SPEAR IS MIKE CHARLIE*.
*MIKE CHARLIE—MISSION CLEAR.

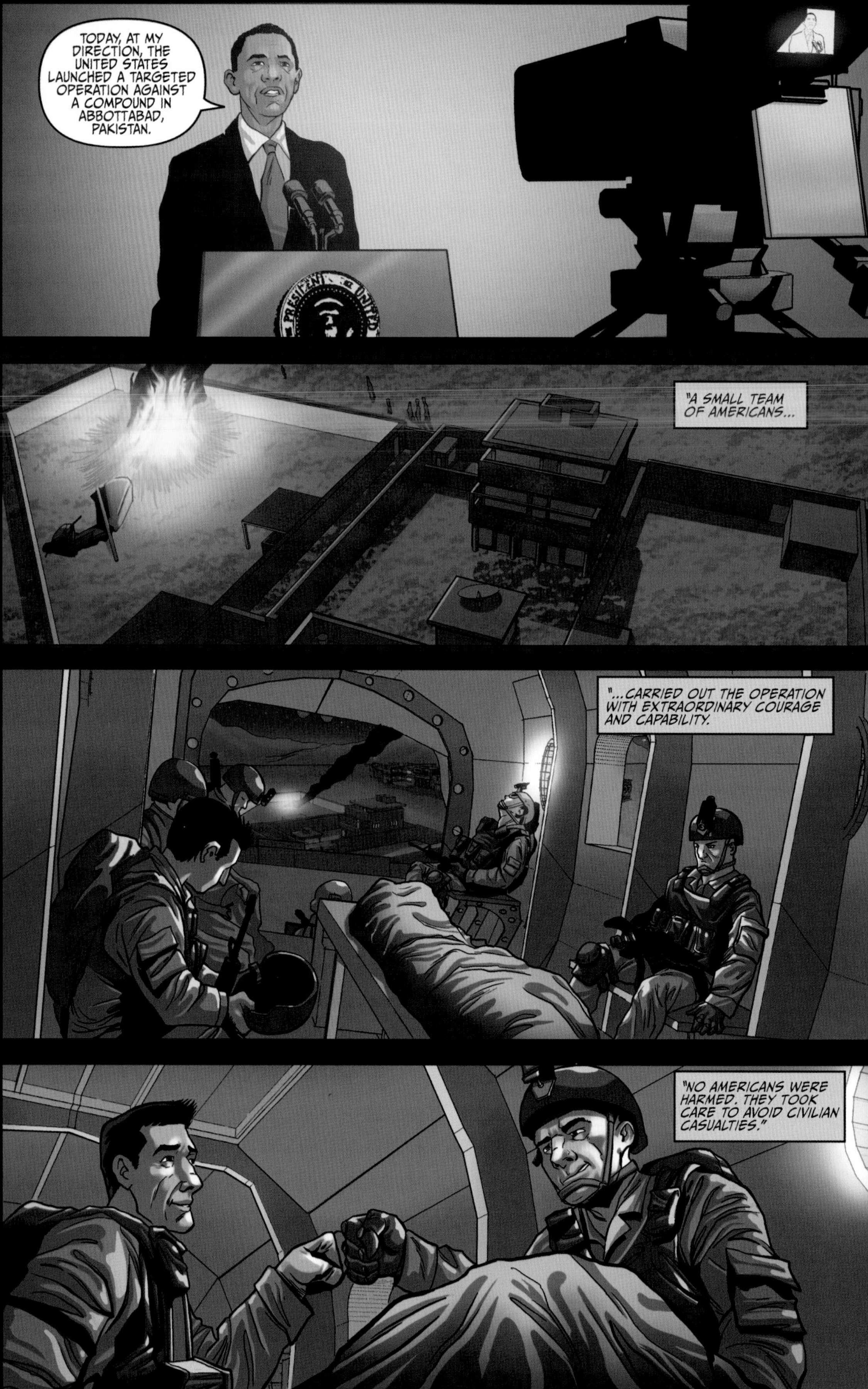
TODAY, AT MY DIRECTION, THE UNITED STATES LAUNCHED A TARGETED OPERATION AGAINST A COMPOUND IN ABBOTTABAD, PAKISTAN.
"A SMALL TEAM OF AMERICANS...
"...CARRIED OUT THE OPERATION WITH EXTRAORDINARY COURAGE AND CAPABILITY.
"NO AMERICANS WERE HARMED. THEY TOOK CARE TO AVOID CIVILIAN CASUALTIES."

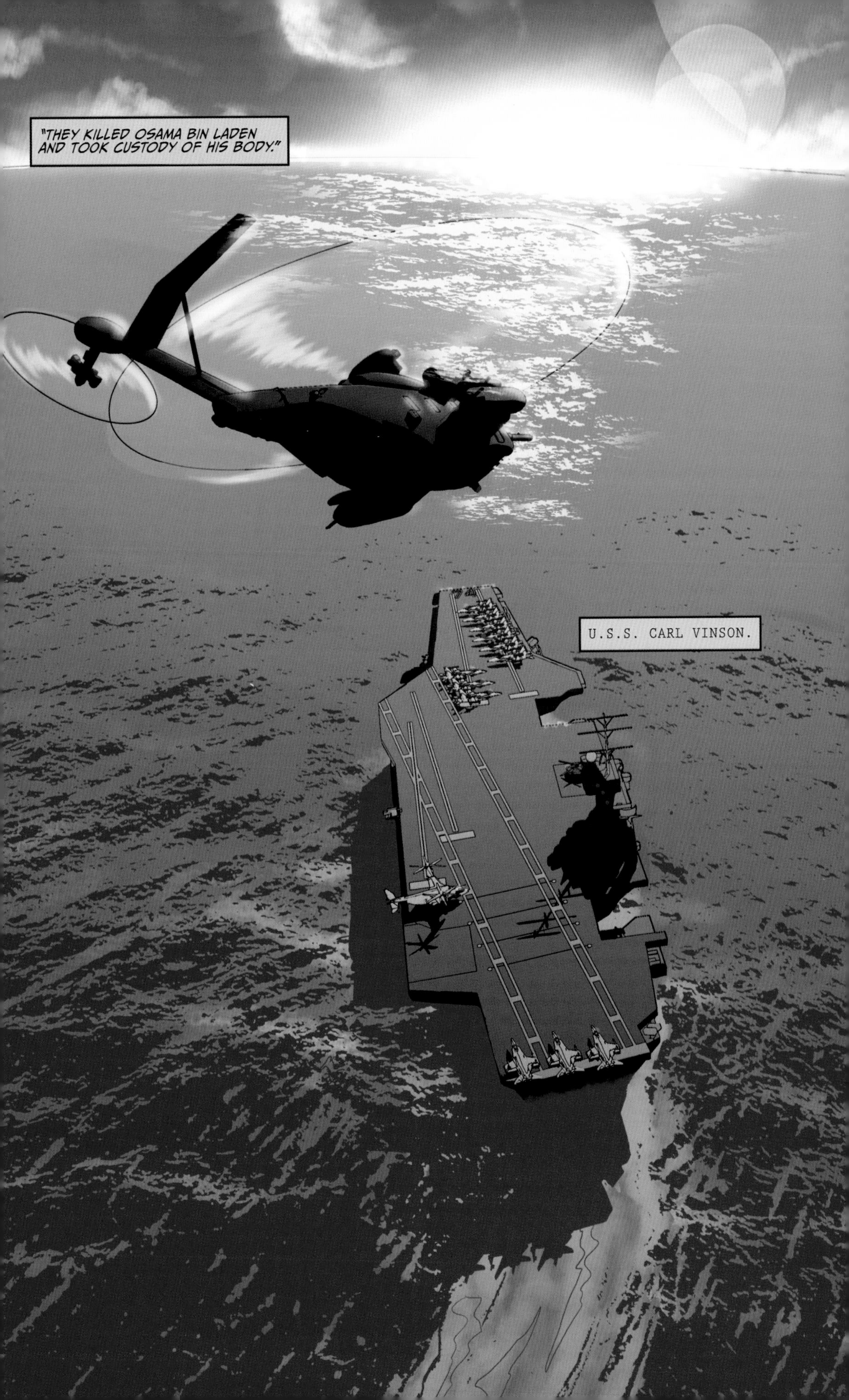
"THEY KILLED OSAMA BIN LADEN AND TOOK CUSTODY OF HIS BODY."
U.S.S. CARL VINSON.

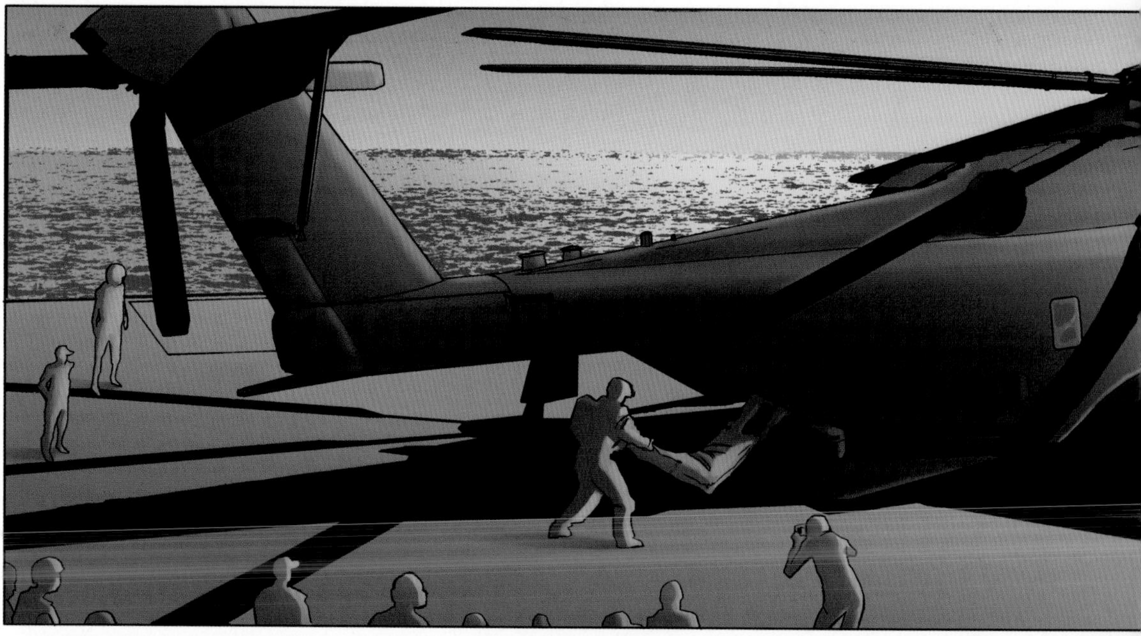

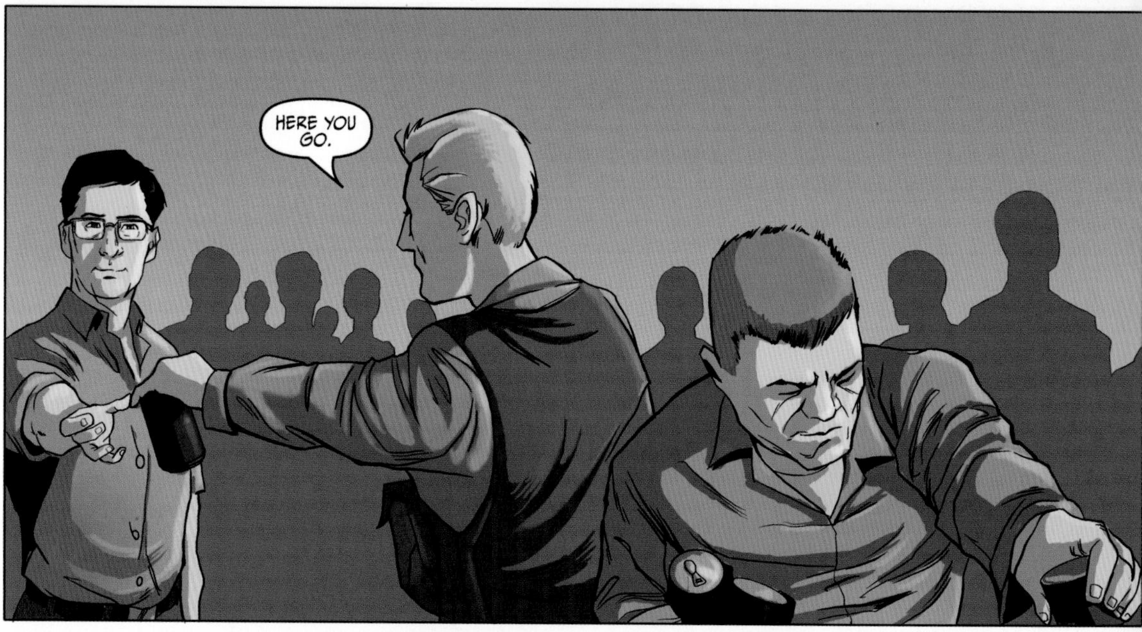
HERE YOU GO.

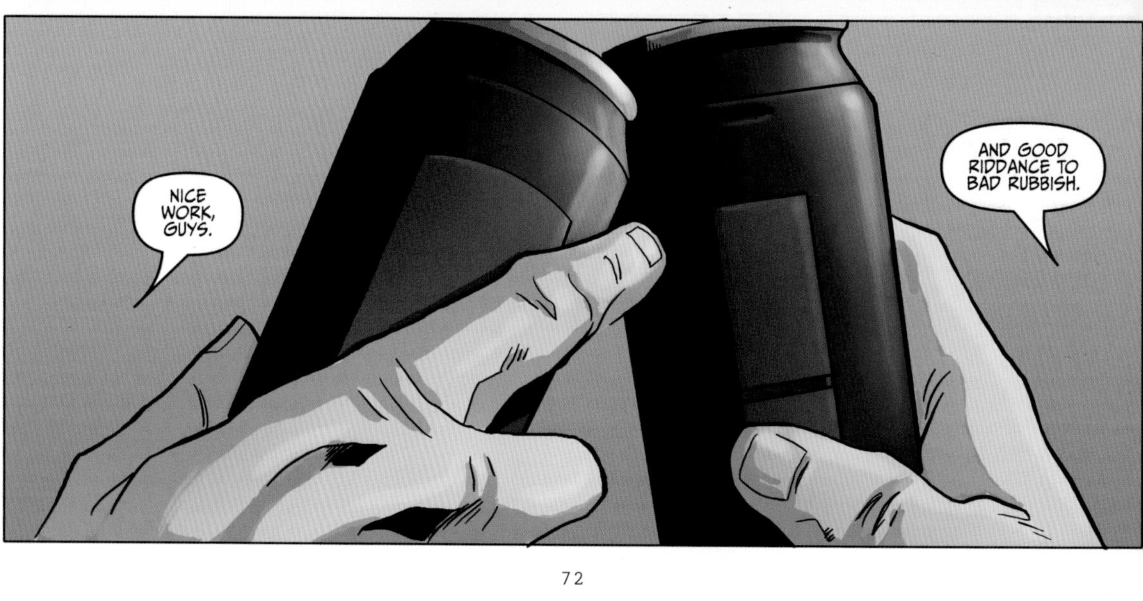
NICE WORK, GUYS.
AND GOOD RIDDANCE TO BAD RUBBISH.

LIVE

AT LONG LAST... AFTER TEN YEARS... WE CAN REPORT THAT OSAMA BIN LADEN... THE SPIRITUAL LEADER OF AL QAEDA AND THE ARCHITECT OF 9-11... IS DEAD.

GNN NEWS

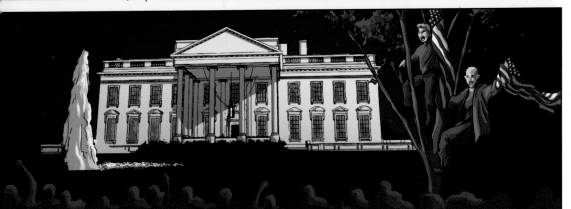

The Washington Post

MONDAY, MAY 2 2011

OSAMA IS DEAD!
AQ Leader killed in daring raid by Navy SEALs.

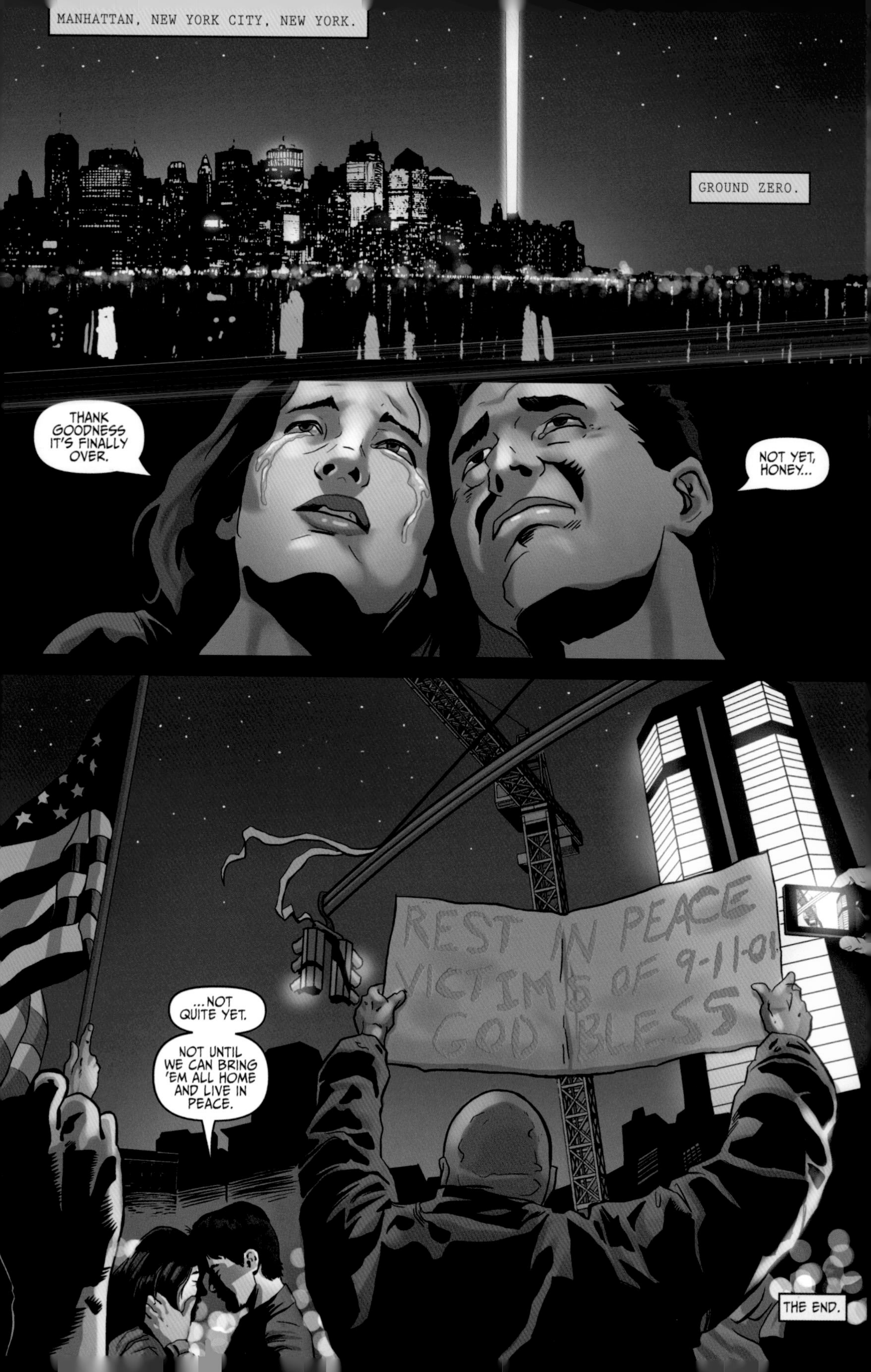
MANHATTAN, NEW YORK CITY, NEW YORK.
GROUND ZERO.
THANK GOODNESS IT'S FINALLY OVER.
NOT YET, HONEY...
REST IN PEACE VICTIMS OF 9-11-01 GOD BLESS
...NOT QUITE YET.
NOT UNTIL WE CAN BRING 'EM ALL HOME AND LIVE IN PEACE.
THE END.

Code Word: Geronimo – Perspectives

By
John M. Del Vecchio

We are the story we tell our selves of ourselves. This is true for individuals and for nations. Story defines us. It creates our self-image. And behavior tends to be consistent with self-image. The story just told is not merely one of skill and valor, of impeccable execution of a military mission, or of the men who carried it out, but it is a story of hope, of optimism, of belief that elements of evil can be defeated and the future can be better than the past. It is an American story.

On May 1, 2011, the leader of SEAL Team 6 uttered, "Geronimo," and the world let out a long-held breath, a sigh of relief. The symbol of ultimate evil was no more. The mission and the team are now legendary. As we further delineate this new American legend, let it bring us closer together.

In light of the controversy surrounding the use of his name, below we take a quick look at Geronimo—the man, the great warrior and chief of the Chiricahua Apache, who raided and evaded encroaching Mexican and American militaries for nearly a third of a century.

Then we look at Osama bin Laden, the Saudi prince, founder and evil director of al-Qaeda, who remotely sent others to raid and sometimes to evade, but more often sacrifice themselves as they terrorized numerous populations around the world.

Next: Who are these amazing SEAL guys?! Holy Toledo! What's their history? How does one qualify? They just pulled off one of the most daring and successful commando raids in American military history—how did they train for it?

And, finally, what does all this mean? What lies ahead? What business remains unfinished? How has the enemy transformed? Is there a message that America, al-Qaeda, and the World should take away from the events of 5/1 to 5/2/11?

Something more than, "Don't Mess With the SEALs!"? Perhaps something about Duty, Honor, Country; something about integrity and remaining forever vigilant; something about dying to make men holy and living to make men free? This is a new element in our legend. This is an American story.

Geronimo – Honor or Insult?

Rage boiled in his belly. It would last for decades. The scene before him was unimaginable. In the darkness he found first one body, then another and another.

Goyathlay and the men of the Chiricahua Apache tribe had left in the early cold of March 6, 1858 to trade at the settlement at Janos in the territory of Chihuahua. Although the Apache and the Mexicans had been at war for centuries, they were now in a period of provisional truce. And, according to Goyathlay's own telling in *Coming of the White Man*, published in 1909, with the

newly arriving White soldiers and settlers, "The Indians always tried to live peaceably." Indeed, when the Americans came, the Apache chiefs met with them and made a treaty. "This was done by shaking hands and promising to be brothers," Goyathlay explained. "Cochise and Mangus-Colorado did likewise. I do not know the name of the officer in command, but this was the first regiment that ever came to Apache Pass."

Late afternoon on that March day in 1858, the sun bore hot upon the return trip of the warriors, and the men were tired from the arduous trek. Before they reached their settlement at Kas-Ki-Yeh, they were intercepted by several women and children of their tribe. These stragglers related a story of terror. A company of 400 Mexican soldiers from Sonora, led by Colonel Jose Maria Carrasco, had surrounded their village. Methodically, the soldiers had killed the few warriors who had remained to guard the tribe. Then, the soldiers moved in and began shooting, pillaging, taking all the ponies, all supplies, and all arms.

Goyathlay and the Apache men, along with the few women and children, dispersed into the sparse, dry lands. After last light, they reassembled in a thicket by the river. Placing sentinels along the way, they stealthily maneuvered back to their village. In the dark, Goyathlay found his aged mother murdered, then his wife, Alope, and all three of their children. He did not speak, did not utter a sound, instead he silently moved back to the river's edge and stared at the water seemingly forever. He and his people had been betrayed. Other warriors came, stood silently with him. The unthinkable had happened. Slowly, they took to motion and gathered for a council. The handshake treaty had been made about a year before the attack on Kas-Ki-Yeh.

Terror spread across the land. Goyathlay was 29 years old. The incident at Kas-Ki-Yeh began his rise to great warrior and chief. The then-chief of his tribe, Mangas-Coloradas, sent him to Cochise for aid in revenging the slaughter. "In a few days after the attack at Apache Pass," Goyathlay wrote years later, "we organized in the mountains and returned to fight the soldiers."

The small band of Apache warriors soon attacked a larger and better-armed contingent of Mexican soldiers. Out-numbered and out-gunned, Goyathlay, oblivious to a barrage of bullets, so viciously attacked with a knife, the routed troops ran screaming appeals to their patron saint, Saint Jerome—in Spanish, *San Jeronimo*. From that day, Goyathlay became known by their prayer: Geronimo.

Geronimo was born on June 16, 1829. For 28 years from the day of the slaughter at Kas-Ki-Yeh, he waged war against the Mexicans and the Americans, defying those who would conquer his people. Battling the shifting sands of time, he became known for his cunning, swift raids, for hasty retreats, and for disappearing into the land. After capture and surrender in 1886, the great warrior and chief became a peacemaker and spokesman for his people.

Some have suggested that the use of the name Geronimo as a code word is a great affront to American Indians. We see it as a great honor to a great man, a great spirit. His name has come to embody the ideals of bravery and valor we ourselves wish to emulate. Indeed, the U.S. military's use of Indian terms is widespread—from Apache, Kiowa and Chinook for helicopters, to Tomahawk for missiles. During World War II, U.S. paratroopers, to instill bravery, yelled as they leapt from their planes, "Geronimo!"

The code name for the Operation at Abbottabad was Neptune Spear. The code word, Geronimo, was not used to mean Osama bin Laden, nor to mean that bin Laden was dead, but was used to designate the 7th or "G" phase of the dangerous mission to find and eliminate bin Laden, and to indicate the raid had accomplished its mission. Geronimo! The evil has been subdued. The most evil of all evil elements that have stalked the earth for the past thirty years is no more.

Osama bin Laden – Not Rage but Hate

Osama bin Mohammad bin Awad bin Laden was born in Riyadh, Saudi Arabia in 1957, one of perhaps 50 children of a rich and powerful man. It is more difficult to imagine his mind and motivation than that of Geronimo's. Bin Laden was not betrayed. His homeland was not besieged. It was not rage boiling in his belly that drove him.

Picture young Osama in the late 1960s and early 1970s. He is a pre-teen living at home with his family. Forget the idea of the poor, the wretched, the disenfranchised. Bin Laden was raised in an affluent area of Jeddah overlooking the Red Sea. Amid the neighborhood of residential compounds were luxury hotels, modern shopping malls, and opulent commercial buildings. The area was a seat of power and influence.

Growing up, Osama watched many hours of TV—was obsessed with news programs. As a ten-year-old, he watched stories about the hijacking of El Al Flight 426 by Palestinian terrorists and the ensuing forty days of negotiations. At fourteen, he watched the murder of Israeli athletes at the Summer Olympic Games in Munich. By this point, he was already an anti-Israel enthusiast. During one show he added his own commentary. His older siblings dismissed his thoughts. To them the uttering was inane. They were a business family. Osama became annoyed. He attempted to rebut, but his siblings did not listen. He attempted to defend himself, but they mocked him then ignored him and walked away. It was not a single incident but one that repeated and became a pattern. The young Saudi resented these dismissals. Disdain grew in his heart. He resented the wealth and power that surrounded him. He scorned the mighty Emirs who had to be obeyed, hated that he buckled under the great power of his own family. Reality, for Osama bin Laden, was this: To be born into a powerful and domineering family was to have no power at all.

Osama bin Laden – Timeline and Atrocities

1976 – At age 18, enters university at Jeddah to study management and economics.

1979 – 26 December: Soviets invade Afghanistan. Five million flee their country and become refugees in Pakistan.

1984 – At age 27, bin Laden uses his management skills to support Arab volunteers arriving in Pakistan to fight the Soviet invasion in the territory to the west.

1986 – bin Laden relocates to Peshawar, Pakistan; forms his own volunteer brigade, imports arms. He is a talented organizer, fund-raiser, and self-promoter. The arms business is lucrative.

1989 – Soviets withdraw from Afghanistan. Bin Laden forms al-Qaeda, which means "The Base," as a movement to attract radical Muslims intent upon imposing fundamentalist governments in their own countries. Bin Laden hones this message, allies with other groups in hatred of the United States, Israel, and any Muslim regimes allied with the U.S. Al-Qaeda soon establishes itself as a trans-national terrorist network with a proactive strategy—it does not merely react to policies or events in the U.S. or other Western democracies. The little boy who had been dismissed by his elder siblings has now become the star of his own show.

1991 – OBL returns to Saudi Arabia; he publically opposes the Saudi alliance with the U.S. against Saddam Hussein, and is exiled to Sudan. He continues morphing from mid-level "management" into international terrorist leader, gaining ever-greater acceptance by espousing a return to the purifying principles of the seventh century Prophet. His writings on the topic are often incoherent, yet his skills as a communicator—aided by the international media and by new electronic technologies, from the Internet to satellite phones—capture the imagination of millions.

1993 – OBL's family formally disenfranchises his interests in the family business.

1994 – In retribution for bin Laden's anti-Saudi propaganda, The Kingdom revokes his citizenship. Osama becomes a man without a country. To his followers, he uses this to play up his martyrdom.

1996 – May: bin Laden is expelled from Sudan. He relocates to Afghanistan.

1996 – August: Osama declares war on the United States, issues a *fatwa* that all U.S. military personnel should be killed.

1996 – September: The Taliban established the Islamic Emirate in Afghanistan.

1996 – October: bin Laden named as prime suspect in bombings in Saudi Arabia, which kills 24 American servicemen.

1996 – 1 November: Al Jazeera initiates its satellite TV news service. Via al-Qaeda's production arm, bin Laden becomes a regular contributor. He refines and polishes his organizational and communication skills. To the Muslim world, he portrays himself as the tall, bearded prince riding a white horse—a Kalashnikov-toting rebel calling for mass violence. The great hope giving voice to the poor, the wretched, the disenchanted, the hopeless.

1996 – The image is manufactured. OBL is part of a very big business. Afghanistan is the world's largest producer of heroin. The Taliban collect a 20% export tax from opium dealers shipping their wares via Iran and Pakistan—this amounts to approximately $500,000,000 in revenue. These funds drive the revolution.

1998 – 7 August: 244 people are killed (12 Americans) as truck bombs explode outside U.S. embassies in Nairobi and Dar es Salaam.

1998 – 20 August: bin Laden named as America's "top enemy" by President Clinton. He is accused of masterminding both embassy bombings. In an attempt to kill bin Laden, the U.S. launches Tomahawk cruise missiles against terrorist bases in the vicinity of Khost, Afghanistan. During a coordinated attack in Sudan, a Khartoum pharmaceutical plant is destroyed—the owner denies any collaboration with bin Laden.

2000 – 12 October: Suicide bombers attack the USS Cole docked at Aden, Yemen. Seventeen American sailors are killed.

2001 – August: al-Qaeda opens secret talks with Pakistani nuclear scientists.

2001 – 11 September: bin Laden's boldest plan is carried out. Hijacked airliners are crashed into the twin towers of New York's World Trade Center and into the Pentagon. A fourth hijacked plane, heading for Washington, D.C., crashes as passengers attempt to wrest control back from terrorists. Approximately 3,000 people are killed. In an al-Qaeda video released shortly thereafter, bin Laden exalts that the collapse of the towers exceeded his expectations.

2001 – 17 September: President George W. Bush declares bin Laden is "Wanted: Dead or Alive."

2001 – November: The Taliban is ousted from power in Afghanistan.

2001 – 6 December: bin Laden's headquarters at Tora Bora in the mountains of Eastern Afghanistan is attacked and captured. Bin Laden escapes. His last will and testament is amongst documents captured. In it, he directs his children <u>not</u> to follow in his work for al-Qaeda, saying, "If it is good, then we have had our share; if it is bad, then it is enough." This is in direct contrast to the memoir of OBL's son Omar, who wrote that his father suggested that he and his brothers should consider becoming suicide bombers for the Taliban. "My father," Omar penned, "hated his enemies more than he loved his sons."

2002 – 10 September: On the eve of the first anniversary of the 9/11/01 attacks, bin Laden, speaking via a recording sent to Al Jazeera, praises the terrorists for "changing the course of history."

2002 – November: fifteen people are killed and 80 wounded at the Mombasa Paradise resort hotel in Kenya. Al-Qaeda claims responsibility.

2002 – During the next several years, OBL repeatedly advocates worldwide Islamic revolution; his credibility as a political figure rises with Muslim populations from Indonesia to Nigeria to nearly fifty percent as he incites the imagination of young fundamentalists.

2004 – In Iraq, on the eve of that nation's first free election, al-Qaeda terrorists change tactics from attacking American targets to attacking Iraqi civilians. Terrorism escalates until the US "surge" specifically targets and eliminates most foreign terrorist cells.

2004 – Over the next six years, al-Qaeda and affiliates plan and carry out violent assaults on civilian and military targets throughout the Middle East, including aiding Hamas in Gaza, and Hezbollah in Lebanon. Other attacks range from Bali to Madrid, London to Marrakech. In Pakistan alone, bin Laden and allied terrorist groups murder 30,000 civilians and 5,000 troops. Although highly organized and developed, under OBL's leadership, al-Qaeda never progresses politically beyond a terrorist organization.

2006 – bin Laden moves into a comfortable, private compound on the outskirts of the garrison town of Abbottabad, Pakistan. To his followers and to the world, he is rumored to be hiding in caves in the Afghan-Pakistani border region of North Waziristan.

2010 – 24 January: In an auto-recording, bin Laden claims responsibility for the failed Christmas Day bombing of a US-bound airliner. He vows to continue attacks against the United States. More threats follow in March as bin Laden threatens to kill any American taken prisoner by al-Qaeda if 9/11 planner Khalid Sheikh Mohammed is executed.

2011 – 21 January: Via released recordings, bin Laden ties the release of French hostages held in Niger by al-Qaeda to the withdrawal of French forces from Muslim countries.

2011 – 1 May [EST, 2 May local time]: bin Laden dispatched by SEAL Team 6; his sanctified remains are dumped from the U.S.S. Carl Vinson into the North Arabian Sea.

2011 – 6 May: bin Laden's death confirmed by al-Qaeda communiqué, which vows revenge.

United States Naval Special Warfare Development Group (NSWDG) or DevGru: SEAL Team 6

So, who are these guys? What's their story? How do they qualify? They just pulled off one of the most daring and successful commando raids in American military history—how did they train for it? What makes them such an amazing band of badass brothers?

As Captain Dye has explained, "Due to entirely appropriate security concerns, there is some creative license in our script." For that same reason, there will be no attempt here to identify anyone; but there will be an attempt to define their qualifications, their training, their character. This book is meant to be a historic tribute commemorating a pivotal moment in history. At the very center of that

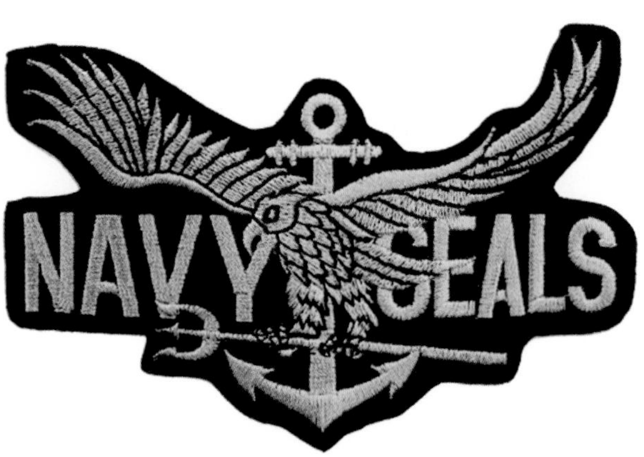
NAVY SEALS

moment is one of America's most secretive, Tier-One, Special Mission Units.

SEAL (Sea, Air and Land) places its origin back in 1962 when President John F. Kennedy was looking for a way to amplify and extend our unconventional warfare force. Indeed, our cultural stories of stealth fighters and derring-do go back much further—back through the air commandos flying the Hump in the China-Burma-India Theater, back through frogmen planting bridge charges along the Rhine, further back through swamp rats and Minutemen. At every stage in our history, a shadowy group of warriors has distinguished themselves and become part of the American legend.

In 1980, after the botched Operation Eagle Claw mission to rescue American hostages from the U.S. Embassy in Iran, the Pentagon recognized the need for a full-time, specifically-dedicated, counter-terrorism unit. From the twelve existing underwater demolition platoons of SEAL Team 1 on the West Coast, two platoons were segregated and tasked with counter-terrorism. After six months of intensive training, this new unit was mission-ready. It became known as Mobility (MOB) 6. In October of that year, it was formally dubbed SEAL Team 6. Like all SEALs, the members are schooled in more conventional warfare applications including underwater demolition, explosive ordinance disposal, and pathfinder responsibilities for amphibious assaults. But SEAL Team 6 goes where no others go—operates in ways no others operate.

The current designation of the unit is Naval Special Warfare Development Group or NAVSPECWARDEVGRU, or simply DevGru (is it any wonder why people still refer to it as SEAL Team 6?!). They have hunted down war criminals in Bosnia, have fought secretive skirmishes in Iraq and Afghanistan, have simultaneously shot Somali pirates in a bobbing craft to rescue American hostage.

Today, DEVGRU is administratively supported by the Naval Special Warfare Command (NAVSPECWARCOM), and is under the operational control of the Joint Special Operations Command (JSOC). It is headquartered at the Training Support Center Hampton Roads, Virginia Beach, Virginia, with a West Coast locus at the Naval Special Warfare Center (NSWC), Coronado, California. DevGru (ST6) draws its personnel from SEAL Teams, but they are not one and the same. DevGru has approximately 300 members; SEAL Teams (1-5, 7-10) total around 2700 personnel. DevGru is specifically tasked (along with the Army's Combat Operations Group [COG], formerly 1st SFOD-D or Delta Force) with counter-terror missions.

All DevGru applicants have passed through BUD/s training (Basic Underwater Demolition School/SEAL), a three-phase, six-month course that makes an NFL training camp look like the Pop Warner league. Hell Week alone, in phase one, is so strenuous with its emphases on running, swimming, crawling through miles of mud, navigating obstacles and lifesaving—non-stop for five days with a total of four hours of sleep—that better than half of all applicants drop out. Those who endure move onto phase two, a seven-week diving course, and then onto the ten-week third phase, which turns them into hardcore naval commandos. But that's just Basic! They are not yet SEALs.

The relaxation of four-weeks of jump school follows: one-week of static line training, then three weeks of Military Free-Fall (MFF). That's the stuff that drops troops behind enemy lines… for some, up to the maximum HALO—high altitude low opening—e.g., a free-fall from 30,000 feet, at night, through clouds, with combat gear, and opening the chute in the last seconds; and HAHO—high altitude high opening, which allows the SEAL to steer his chute to an LZ up to 25 miles from his aircraft exit! But still not SEALs!

The candidate now returns for an additional 20 weeks of more brutal preparation—the SQT, or SEAL Qualification Training course. It is not until after the successful completion of SQT that a trainee officially becomes a SEAL and is entitled to wear the Trident emblem—while he is on probation for 18 months with a SEAL team.

From the pool of SEALs, DevGru candidates are chosen. Criteria include combat experience with a proven record under fire, language skills to interact with foreign nationals, along with the ability to blend in with the civilian population during covert operations. These are America's best and brightest sons. Every man brings a different set of abilities; all bring close-quarter combat skills, an array of maritime, ground and airborne tactics, and the skill of being able to work as a team. These levels of proficiency and competence require years of training and experience. Most DevGru members are in their 30s, significantly older than the average sailor. A candidate chosen for DevGru spends his first six to seven months in even more advanced training—the Operators Training Course—free-climbing, advanced unarmed combat, defensive and offensive driving, advanced diving, survival, evasion, resistance and escape techniques. Along with the skills and mechanics, they learn the art and philosophy of warfare. Most importantly, they learn the absolute limits of their own being.

SEAL Team 6 originally was mandated with worldwide, maritime counter-terrorism responsibilities, including objectives such as ships, oilrigs, naval bases and civilian ports. Some members are tasked with infiltrating and reconnoitering international hot spots, others with security assessments of U.S. embassies. DevGru's mission includes pre-emptive and pro-active counter-terrorism and counter-proliferation operations. At times, it operates with the Army's Combat Operations Group (COG) as part of a joint special task force, or with the CIA's Special Activities Division (SAD) and Special Operations Group (SOG).

In the month leading up to Operation Neptune Spear, DevGru's Red Squadron from Dam Neck, Virginia used replicas of bin Laden's compound, first at bases on both American coasts, then in a restricted section of Camp Alpha at Bagram Airbase in Afghanistan, to simulate its assault. Modified MH-60 helicopters from the U.S. Army's 160th Special Operations Aviation Regiment… well, that's all in the illustrated story just told.

Character

A team's character is forged in sweat, is finely honed to a cohesive fighting edge designed for battle through the extremes of training and experience. A man's character has many elements, many forces have to shape it. To be a DevGru SEAL requires strength, stamina, confidence, discipline, intelligence, integrity and spirit. A crucial fire must burn in one's belly to be willing to sacrifice all for the success of the mission. Character includes the drive to gain the knowledge and experience of a vast array of equipment and weapons, and the will to use that vast array of equipment, the will to intelligently use lethal force in complex and potentially ambiguous situations.

Upon his death in 1964, the family of General Douglas MacArthur released a prayer he wrote for his son in 1942. It is partially quoted below. Today we might wish to think of it as America writing to its military "sons," perhaps describing the character of its SEALs.

"Build me a son, O Lord, who will be strong enough to know when he is weak, and brave enough to face himself when he is afraid; one who will be proud and unbending in honest defeat, and humble and gentle in victory… Build me a son whose heart will be clear, whose goal will be high; a son who will master himself before he seeks to master other men; one who will learn to laugh, yet never forget how to weep; one who will reach into the future, yet never forget the past…"

Perspectives – Lessons Learned; Unfinished Business; Closure

In the introduction, we asked, "What does all this mean? What lies ahead? How has the enemy been transformed? How franchised? Is there a message that America, al-Qaeda, and the world should take away from the events of 5/1 to 5/2/11? Something more than, "Don't Mess With the SEALs!" (…which, as we've seen, is not a bad lesson to learn).

Now that Osama bin Laden is dead and, in the words of President Barack Obama, "Justice has been served," which future course should we follow? Which policies will best keep us from future attack? Options are easy to generate, and political expediency may determine the road ahead, but to keep faith with the spirit of those who undertook Operation Neptune Spear, let us briefly explore a few of those options and project a few potential ramifications.

Osama bin Laden formed al-Qaeda in Afghanistan in the late 1980s, and much of our reaction, our *War on Terror*, targeted his organization. But long ago, al-Qaeda metastasized. Cells developed in Waziristan, in Peshawar, in Yemen, in Indonesia, in European ghettos, in American suburbs. In Pakistan—perhaps the mother nest of Islamic terrorism—al-Qaeda allied with the Taliban, the Haqqani network, Hizb-i-Islami, Lashkar-e-Jhangvi (anti-Shiite), Lashkar-e-Taiba (LET, now Jamaat ul-Dawa—anti-Kashmir), and separatist groups from Chechnya and Uzbekistan to the Philippines. To understand the history and the extent of these movements requires an entire library—hopefully one our leaders will read. But just as we are the story of ourselves, understand that there is an Islamist narrative with which the behavior of adherents is consistent.

Of the nearly 25,000 Pakistani madrassas—religious schools designed to educate and graduate Islamic clerics—at least 15% are suspected of being radical. Fifteen percent means approximately 150,000 students drilled in Jihadi extremism spreading their insidious doctrine of sectarian violence via an assortment of media and means. This is in a nation of 180 million people; a nation armed with at least 100 nuclear weapons; a nation whose current government, a long-term, putative U.S. ally (we've given them tens of billions of dollars since 9/11), is likely corrupt, certainly troubled, potentially unstable. Extremist and terrorist groups appear to enjoy immunity from the law. The potential is real for the government to be replaced by a theocratic regime akin to that in Iran.

In Afghanistan, the situation, because of the presence of American and allied troops, is, at least on the surface, far more stable. There is still corruption—it is reported that the opium trade alone annually generates over two trillion dollars in revenue, and that war profiteering is rampant. So why do we stay? Why do we expend this effort, this commitment in blood and treasure? Should the death of bin Laden accelerate the withdrawal of American and allied troops from Afghanistan? Or do we yet have unfinished business?

The threat of future violence spewing from the region has not been extinguished. Three occasions come to mind in which withdrawal created power vacuums and lead directly to renewed violence. In 1949, during the sigh of relief following World War II, we withdrew our troops from Korea and Kim Il Sung moved his forces south; in 1972, Hanoi interpreted our withdrawals from South Viet Nam as the okay to attack in force—the Easter Offensive ensued; and, in 1989, after the Soviet defeat in Afghanistan, we essentially abandoned the battlefield to the Taliban, allowing that regime and various terrorist factions a haven in which to thrive.

Our military presence is a great deterrent to aggressors and terrorists. It disrupts their operations and forces them to defend their bases. Also, withdrawals are, on the part of a nation that withdraws, a signal to the population and its media to turn their attention elsewhere. Consider Southeast Asia in 1973 and 1974 when news coverage dropped to less than 1% of the stories broadcast in 1969 and the lack of focus, along with the final withdrawal in 1975, lead to genocides; or Iraq today—although that story is still unfolding. When we are no longer engaged, we tend to be no longer vigilant... a condition which invites aggression's resurgence.

It is a balancing act. Intervention has its limits. Being vigilant does not necessitate the status quo. For example, if billions of dollars are paid to the Pakistani military to hunt down terrorists, shouldn't we explore the economic incentive of harboring terrorists, the symbiotic relationship which inures terrorist communities? If the Pakistani's were completely successful in their anti-terrorist efforts, would the funds be cut off? Just as in the '50s, '60s, and '70s one should not have separated Cambodia and Laos from Viet Nam because the military and terrorist forces were regional, one today cannot separate Afghanistan, or Afghanistan and Pakistan, from a regional solution. An overly rapid withdrawal from Afghanistan, besides perhaps allowing gains within that country to be reversed, may destabilize Pakistan. Repercussions would be felt from India through Iran, to Iraq, Syria, and across North Africa. Likely much further.

The story *Code Word: Geronimo* is an American story. Osama bin Laden is dead. Though we celebrate the action and the results, the celebration is not joyous. The demise of the founder of al-Qaeda does not return to us those he has murdered. It does not reinstate freedoms lost due to the implementation of more invasive security and surveillance infrastructures. It may take a generation to assimilate the changes to our culture.

In the words of President Obama, "On September 11, 2001, in our time of grief, the American people came together. We offered our neighbors a hand, and we offered the wounded our blood. We reaffirmed our ties to each other and our love of community and country."

As a people we have just witnessed an entire operation—from the intelligence services to the support elements to the boots on the ground—which demonstrated American exceptionalism. Let us rededicate ourselves to each other, to America, to the Spirit of Duty, Honor, and Country. Let us remain forever vigilant, and forever looking out for one another. Let us radiate our core values of honesty and integrity; let us be faithful to the public trust. The scars will always be there, but let our post-traumatic growth leave us—as individuals and as a nation—stronger.

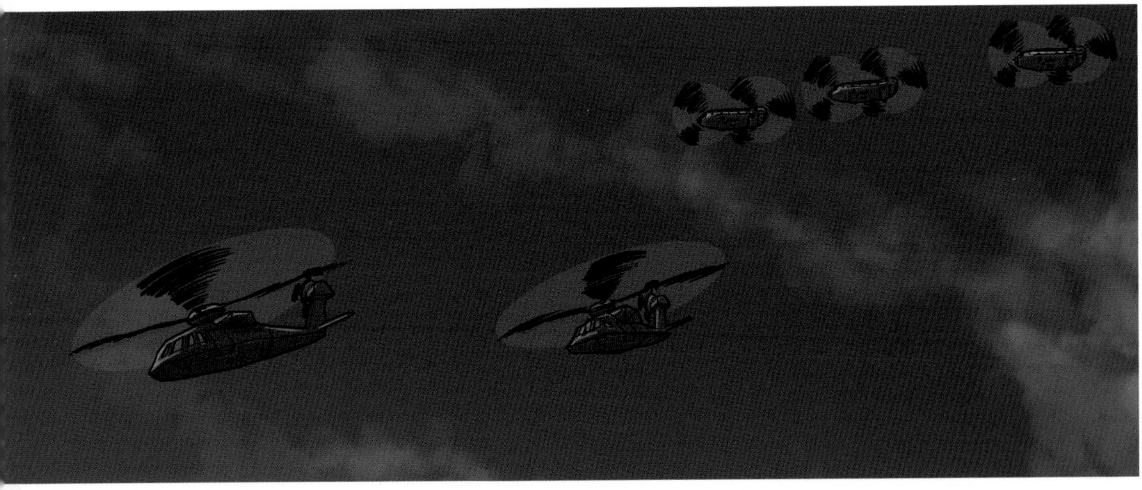

FROM THE GREATEST GENERATION
TO THE LATEST GENERATION

IDW Publishing and Charlie Foxtrot Entertainment are proud to donate a portion of the proceeds from **Code Word: Geronimo** to the **American Veterans Center**, whose stated mission "is to preserve and promote the legacy of America's servicemen and women from World War II through Operation Iraqi Freedom."

To learn more about the **American Veterans Center**, please visit them on the Internet at **www.americanveteranscenter.org**.

CREATOR BIOGRAPHIES

Captain Dale A. Dye, USMC (Ret) was born in Cape Girardeau, Missouri. He graduated as a cadet officer from Missouri Military Academy but there was no money for college so he enlisted in the United States Marine Corps in January 1964. He served in Vietnam in 1965 and 1967 through 1970, surviving 31 major combat operations. He emerged from Southeast Asia highly decorated, including three Purple Hearts for wounds suffered in combat. He spent 13 years as an enlisted Marine, rising to the rank of Master Sergeant before he was chosen to attend Officer Candidate School. Appointed a Warrant Officer in 1976, he later converted his commission and was a Captain when he was sent to Beirut with the Multinational Peacekeeping Force in 1982-83. He served in a variety of assignments around the world and along the way managed to graduate with a B.A. degree in English from the University of Maryland. Dye worked for a year at *Soldier of Fortune Magazine* and spent time in Central America, reporting and training troops in guerrilla warfare techniques in both El Salvador and Nicaragua before leaving the magazine in 1985 and heading for Hollywood, where he founded Warriors, Inc., the leading military consultancy to the entertainment industry. His firm has worked on more than 50 films and TV shows including several Academy Award and Emmy-winning productions, working closely with the directors and actors on almost every major war film to come out of Hollywood in the last 23 years. Dye directed the 2nd unit of *Alexander* under Oliver Stone, and used his influence on the maxi-series *The Pacific* for HBO. He is currently in pre-production on his feature-film directorial debut, *No Better Place to Die*.

Julia Dye, Ph.D. keeps the Entertainment Industry honest through technical advising and performer training, and helps Hollywood directors capture the realities of warfare in all aspects of the media. As a partner in the consulting firm Warriors, Inc., she provided weapons training to Colin Farrell for the film *Alexander* and with the military advisory team, oversaw historical accuracy for the HBO series, *The Pacific*. Dye earned her doctorate in hoplology (the anthropology of human conflict) from The Union Institute & University. She is a frequent consultant for the History Channel, Military Channel and Discovery Channel and is the former Executive Director of the Society of American Fight Directors, and helped create the Los Angeles Fight Academy.

John M. Del Vecchio is a best-selling author, specializing in books on the war in Southeast Asia and the veteran homecoming experience. He was drafted in 1969 shortly after graduating from Lafayette College with a Bachelors Degree in Psychology and minor emphasis in Civil engineering. In 1970, he volunteered for Viet Nam where he served as combat correspondent for the 101st Airborne Division (Airmobile). In 1971, he was awarded a Bronze Star for Heroism in Ground Combat. He is author of *The 13th Valley*, *For the Sake of All Living Things*, *Carry Me Home*, and *Darkness Falls*, along with numerous articles and papers. *The 13th Valley* was a million+ copy bestseller,

Gerry Kissell started his professional career in 1986 as the full time illustrator for *Selling Power Magazine*, the #1 sales and marketing magazine in the United States. His first comic strip was so well received it was picked up by Reuters and published in their internal company newsletter. In 1990, Gerry left his art career to serve his country during the first Gulf War. After his return to civilian life, he didn't miss a beat, creating for FXM, Inc., two limited edition *Star Trek* art prints that sold out within two months. Since then, Gerry has worked for IDW Publishing on *The A-Team: War Stories*, as well as EA Games comic division, working on the *Army of Two* comic series. He has also painted book covers for Warriors Publishing Group, including the new covers for the bestselling novels *The 13th Valley* by John M. Del Vecchio, and *Outrage* by Captain Dale Dye. In 2011, he joined forces with fellow artist Amin Amat to form Hazmat Studios, where their slogan is, "Art so amazing, its hazardous to your health."

Amin Amat is a comic book artist currently living in San Juan, Puerto Rico. An alumni from the School of Visual Arts NYC, he has worked with such notable companies as Moonstone Books, Penny Farthing Press, Marvel Interactive, Coca-Cola, Disney, Scholastic Books, and IDW Publishing. He has contributed to such titles as *Karl Kolchak: The Night Stalker* and *Buckaroo Banzai*.